The Creative Teacher

SECOND EDITION

**Steve Springer, MA,
Brandy Alexander, MFA,
and Kimberly Persiani, EdD**

McGraw Hill Education

New York Chicago San Francisco Athens London Madrid
Mexico City Milan New Delhi Singapore Sydney Toronto

1 2 3 4 5 6 7 8 9 10 11 12 13 14 15 16 17   QVS/QVS   1 0 9 8 7 6 5 4 3

ISBN   978-0-07-180109-6 (Book and CD set)
MHID   0-07-180109-X

ISBN   978-0-07-180110-2 (Book for set)
MHID   0-07-180110-3

e-ISBN   978-0-07-183965-5
e-MHID   0-07-183965-8

Library of Congress Control Number 2012938188

McGraw-Hill Education products are available at special quantity discounts to use as premiums and sales promotions or for use in corporate training programs. To contact a representative, please visit the Contact Us pages at www.mhprofessional.com.

This book is printed on acid-free paper.

Contents

Contents

Preface

In this second edition of *The Creative Teacher*, we included the new ideas we generated but could not fit into our first edition. We also wanted to incorporate feedback from other teachers who have reviewed the book and/or asked us to include specific ideas. This book is meant as a one-stop resource for teachers who need immediate ideas to make their curriculum more relevant and engaging. It also includes fresh concepts for educators searching for something different from and more interesting than what they have been using.

With these goals in mind, writing this book was as simple as referring to the many boxes, files, and resource books we have gathered; websites we visited; and workshops and conferences we attended over the years. More than anything, we wanted to organize a resource to help teachers make their curriculum come to life. *The Creative Teacher* does just that.

Being teachers ourselves, we developed a list of the many resources we wished we had had at our fingertips for our own classrooms. We also discussed key areas that we felt were left out of many curriculums. It seemed that there was never enough time or we didn't have enough information to do justice to certain curricular areas, such as book reports, math reviews, social studies research reports, simple science experiments, art projects, and essay writing. We believe that if there is one resource teachers can consult for such ideas, there will be less need for stacks of supplemental materials, which busy teachers rarely have time for.

Revisiting this book was a great experience, and we hope that new and veteran teachers will find it useful in preparing their curriculum throughout the year. We continue to add creative ideas to our own repertoire including resources such as teacher-made worksheets, puppets, report guidelines, workshop tips, as well as the wonderful ideas we have collected from colleagues, students in our teacher preparation programs, and our current student teachers. We recognize that there are many amazing books available to help new and veteran teachers, but we also know how important this book will be in combining these ideas offering a one-stop resource.

Kimberly Persiani, EdD
Associate Professor
CSU, Los Angeles

Introduction

"The ultimate freedom for creative groups is the freedom to experiment with new ideas. Some skeptics insist that innovation is expensive. In the long run, innovation is cheap. Mediocrity is expensive—and autonomy can be the antidote." Tom Kelly, General Manager, IDEO
> —Daniel H. Pink, *Drive: The Surprising Truth About What Motivates Us*

Many teachers still believe that the best way to motivate students is with rewards and incentives, but Daniel Pink would likely say that's a mistake. He proclaims that the secret to high performance and satisfaction at school is the deeply human need to direct our own lives, to learn and create new things, and to do better by ourselves and our world. The second edition of *The Creative Teacher* holds this thought at the forefront as we offer a variety of subject-specific activities that not only tap into the Common Core Standards (CCS) but also push for creativity, innovation, autonomy, critical thinking, and inference to encourage those new ideas and avoid the mediocrity that Daniel Pink speaks of.

Why a Second Edition?

With the Common Core Standards coming into play, and the 21st century well under way, this is the perfect time for us to revisit and update the first edition. We also offer new and interesting ideas to not only meet the demands of the CCSs but also the demands of the advancements in digital media as well as the ever-changing diverse student population.

What's New?

One of the most important aspects of the second edition is that the template pages will now be available for download for ease of use when planning lessons. New templates to help support activities throughout the book will also be made accessible for corresponding pages. These templates will be noted by the CD icon, which serves to remind you that there is a template ready for your students' use.

In this edition, you will find a variety of updated activities, such as new book reports, including one for creating a Social Network Profile page on story characters or real people from informational texts. Other responses to literature in the Book Reports section offer the options of predicting the future through the "Crystal Ball," digging around in a story character's garbage in "Take Out the Trash," and solving problems in the story by writing to "Dear Abby."

Teachers will be excited to see new Graphic Organizers to help students keep track of data for writing essays. Some are related to types of writing, such as compare and contrast; developing topic ideas for stories; or preparing information to write history and/or science reports.

Other areas to find new templates and new activities include science. You will enjoy teaching your students how to create a terrarium with products they can bring from home. Also included is an ever-popular social studies assignment that asks students to create a flag or re-create one for a country they are studying or where their family originates from. And several new art activities are added. A student favorite is creating tissue paper scenes, settings, or locations for geography, stories being read in class, or places they'd like to visit someday. Another art lesson gives students a chance at creativity by making a collage. These can be used to model a historical figure, a scene or setting from a story, or a geographic location.

This book also lends itself to meeting elements of the Common Core Standards. The Mission of the Common Core Standards states:

> The Common Core State Standards provide a consistent, clear understanding of what students are expected to learn, so teachers and parents know what they need to do to help them. The standards are designed to be robust and relevant to the real world, reflecting the knowledge and skills that our young people need for success in college and careers. With American students fully prepared for the future, our communities will be best positioned to compete successfully in the global economy.
> (http://www.corestandards.org/)

The Common Core State Standards Initiative is a state-led effort coordinated by the National Governors Association Center for Best Practices (NGA Center) and the Council of Chief State School Officers (CCSSO). The standards were developed in collaboration with teachers, school administrators, and experts to provide a clear and consistent framework to prepare our children for college and the workforce.

The standards are informed by the highest, most effective models from across the United States and around the world, and they provide teachers and parents with a common understanding of what students are expected to learn. Consistent standards will provide appropriate benchmarks for all students, regardless of where they live.

These standards define the knowledge and skills students should have within their K–12 education careers so that they will graduate high school able to succeed in entry-level, credit-bearing academic college courses and in workforce training programs. The standards:

- Align with college and work expectations
- Are clear, understandable, and consistent
- Include rigorous content and application of knowledge through high-order skills
- Build upon strengths and lessons of current state standards
- Are informed by other top performing countries, so that all students are prepared to succeed in our global economy and society
- Are evidence-based (http://www.corestandards.org/about-the-standards)

It is with great pride that we offer you this new edition.

Book Reports

This chapter includes a variety of book report formats ranging from a few sentences for the early grades, to deeper inference and higher level prompts for the upper grades. Encouraging a combination of fiction and nonfiction texts allows for creativity and student choice while also meeting the Common Core Standards for English Language Arts and Literacy.* As students advance through the grades and master grade level standards in reading, writing, speaking, listening, and language, they are able to exhibit the following as literate individuals:

1. They demonstrate independence.
2. They build strong content knowledge.
3. They respond to the varying demands of audience, task, purpose, and discipline.
4. They comprehend as well as critique.
5. They value evidence.
6. They use technology and digital media strategically and capably.
7. They come to understand other perspectives and cultures.

All of this can be accomplished when consistently incorporating Book Reports and responses to literature into your curriculum.

_____

*To read the Common Core Standards in more detail and to obtain the grade level specific standards for English Language Arts and Literacy, visit http://www.corestandards.org.

Submarine Sandwich

Grades 3–12

Materials Needed

Ham—pink construction paper
Lettuce—green construction paper
Tomato—red construction paper
Cheese—orange construction paper
Mayonnaise—white construction paper
Mustard—yellow construction paper
Bread—beige (top and bottom pieces)
Brad to hold the submarine sandwich together
Crayons/colored pencils/pens

Student Guidelines

1. On the top slice of bread, students will write the title of the book, the author, the illustrator (if applicable), the publisher, and the copyright date. This will teach the student how, what, and where to look for these elements in every book they use.
2. On the mustard, students will write a summary of the book, including the sequence of events for the reader to follow.
3. On the lettuce, students will describe the main characters in detail, including physical characteristics if applicable, their dispositions/personalities, their role in the book, and whether or not students might be friends with these characters in real life along with an explanation as to why or why not.
4. On the ham, students will describe the setting of the book.
5. On the cheese, students will describe the turning point, or climax, of the book.
6. On the tomato, students will list and define five unfamiliar words from the book.
7. On the mayonnaise, students will draw a picture of a specific scene in the book that depicts an understanding of the plot.
8. On the bottom slice of bread, students will write their name as "Written by. . . ."
9. Connect all of the submarine sandwich ingredients together at one end with the brad.

   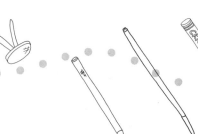

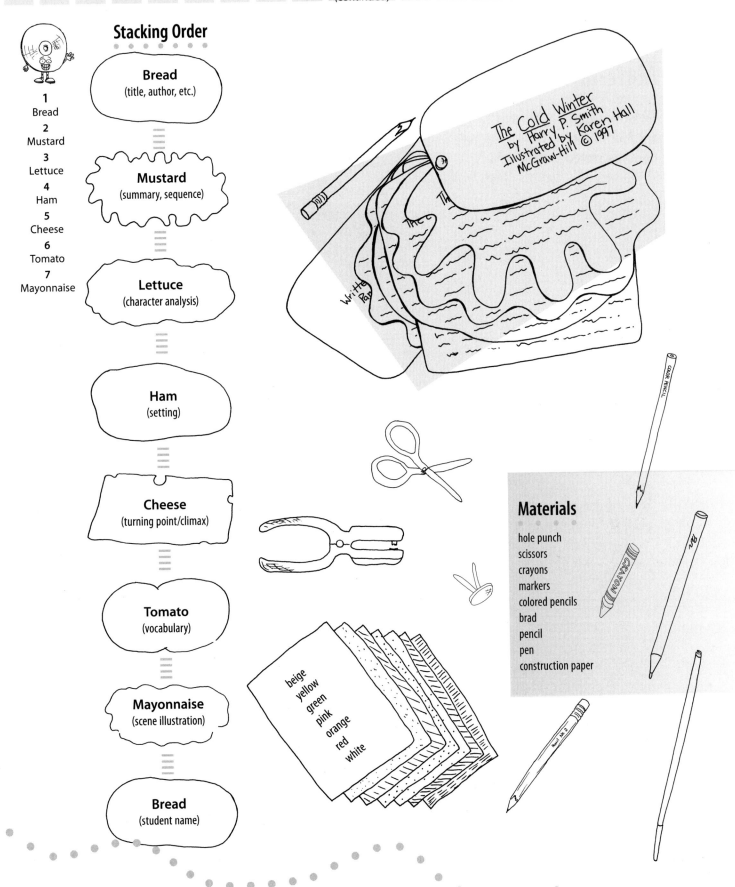

Stacking Order

1 Bread
2 Mustard
3 Lettuce
4 Ham
5 Cheese
6 Tomato
7 Mayonnaise

Bread
(title, author, etc.)

Mustard
(summary, sequence)

Lettuce
(character analysis)

Ham
(setting)

Cheese
(turning point/climax)

Tomato
(vocabulary)

Mayonnaise
(scene illustration)

Bread
(student name)

Materials

hole punch
scissors
crayons
markers
colored pencils
brad
pencil
pen
construction paper

beige
yellow
green
pink
orange
red
white

The Cold Winter
by Harry P. Smith
Illustrated by Karen Hall
McGraw-Hill © 1997

Lunch Bag

Grades 4–12

Materials Needed

Brown lunch bag
5 × 7 index cards
Crayons/colored pencils/pens

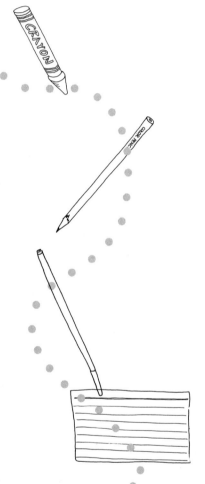

Student Guidelines

- Compile 10 index cards. On each card, students will list a question and its answer on the front. On the back, they will illustrate the situation. Five of the questions need to be directly related to the content of the story. These might include but are not limited to setting, conflicts, turning point in the story, and so on. Five of the questions need to be inference questions.
- Using index cards, create a 10-word glossary of unfamiliar words from the book. Along with writing a definition for each word, students will write the corresponding sentence from the book and a sentence of their own.
- On index cards, describe each of the characters. Include their physical characteristics if applicable, and then describe their personalities and their roles in the book.
- On the outside front of the brown bag, illustrate one of the major scenes from the book. Add the book's title, author, illustrator, publisher, and copyright date.
- On the outside back of the brown bag, write your name.
- Place the index cards into the brown bag and deliver to the teacher as if it were a lunch.

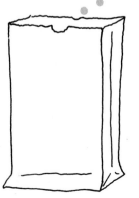

Note: This can also be done with shoe boxes, manila envelopes, cereal boxes, and similar items.

10 Total Questions/Answers

5—direct content

5—inference

10-Word Glossary

sentences

Character Descriptions

FRONT

BACK

Book Critic

Grades 3–12

Materials Needed

Examples of newspaper book or movie reviews
White construction paper
Lined paper
Crayons/colored pencils/pens

Student Guidelines

- On the construction paper, students will illustrate the plot scene from their book. Above the picture, students will write the title, author, illustrator (if applicable), the publisher, and the copyright date.
- Using the book and movie review examples, students will write a review about their book as if it were to be published in the Sunday edition of the newspaper.
- In the review, students should focus on the believability of the book, the characters' personalities, and the plot conflict/resolution as well as the major turning point in the story line.
- Students will give the audience a thumbs-up or thumbs-down on the book, explaining their reasoning.
- This can be done in pairs if two students read the same book.
- The illustration can be attached to the front of the book review.

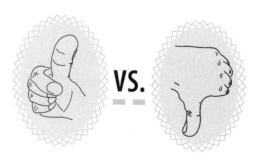

VS.

Name: _____ Date: _____

Use this template to create a one-page book review. Consider including the following: title, author, genre, character/s, plot, setting, problem, solution, and recommendation with an explanation.

CLASS TIMES

BOOK REVIEW

By _____

_____

_____

_____

_____

_____

_____

_____

_____

_____

_____

_____

_____

_____

Illustrate a scene from your favorite part of the book.

_____

_____

_____

_____

_____

_____

_____

_____

Book Jacket
Grades 1–12

Materials Needed

White construction paper
Crayons/colored pencils/pens

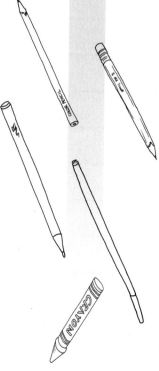

Student Guidelines

- Fold the construction paper in fourths. The two edge flaps serve as the inside book flaps. The two inner sections serve as the front and back covers of the book.
- On the front cover, illustrate a major scene from the book. Include the title, author, illustrator (if applicable), publisher, and copyright date.
- On the front inside flap, include a summary of the book in sequence. This should include the setting, the plot, and the climax of the story—the conflict and resolution.
- On the back inside flap, describe the main characters of the story in as much detail as possible, including their physical characteristics if available, their personalities, and their roles in the story.
- On the back cover, list 5 to 10 quotes from the story that convey an understanding of the plot.

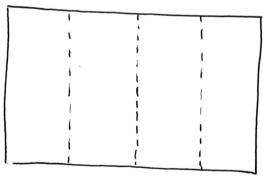

Fold paper in half and then in half again.

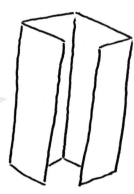

Book Jacket

Inside Front Flap

Summary—in sequence
(setting, plot, climax, conflict, resolution)

Front Cover

Illustration—major scene
(title, author, illustrator, publisher, copyright)

Inside Back Flap

Description—main characters
(physical characteristics, personalities, roles)

Back Cover

Quotes—from text
(5–10 showing understanding of plot)

Cookin' Up Books
Grades 1–12

Materials Needed

Recipe template
Crayons/colored pencils/markers/pencils/pens
Hole punch
Twist tie

Student Guidelines

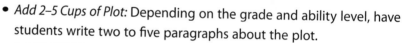

- *Add 2–5 Cups of Plot:* Depending on the grade and ability level, have students write two to five paragraphs about the plot.
- *Add 2–5 Tablespoons of Characters:* Have students describe the characters, including physical characteristics, if applicable, and personality traits as well as each character's role in the story. The number of characters/ tablespoons depends on the book and grade/ability level of the students.
- *Add 2–5 Teaspoons of Information:* Have students select two to five passages or quotes from their books that depict main scenes from the story. The students should try to include passages or quotes that portray the main characters and/or plotline.
- *Mix Ingredients Together:* When cool, frost with the following icing:
  - *1 Cup of Opinion*—What did you like or not like about the book? Use specific examples from the story.
  - *1 Tablespoon of Recommendation*—Would you encourage your friends to read this book? Why or why not? Be critical of the book and very specific about who this book would entertain the most.
- *Decorate:* Sprinkle the following information:

Title of Book	Name of Illustrator
Name of Author	Copyright Date
Name of Publisher	

Sample Report

Student Heading

Plot
2–3 paragraphs

Characters
characteristics, personalities, roles

Information
passages/quotes portraying main characters

Opinion
examples

**Poster Board/
Large Construction Paper**

Recommendation

**Title
Author
Publisher
Illustrator
Copyright**

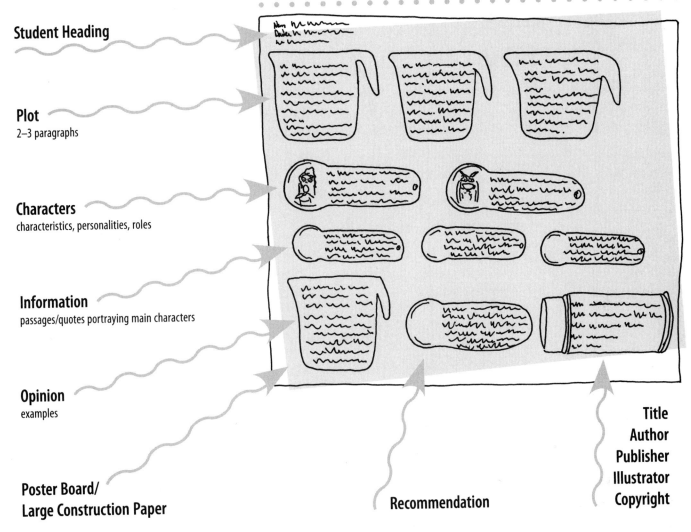

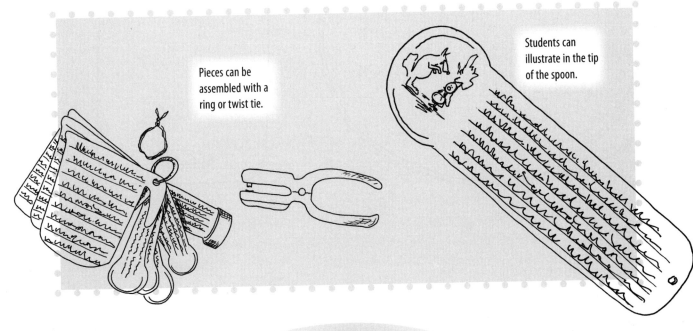

Pieces can be assembled with a ring or twist tie.

Students can illustrate in the tip of the spoon.

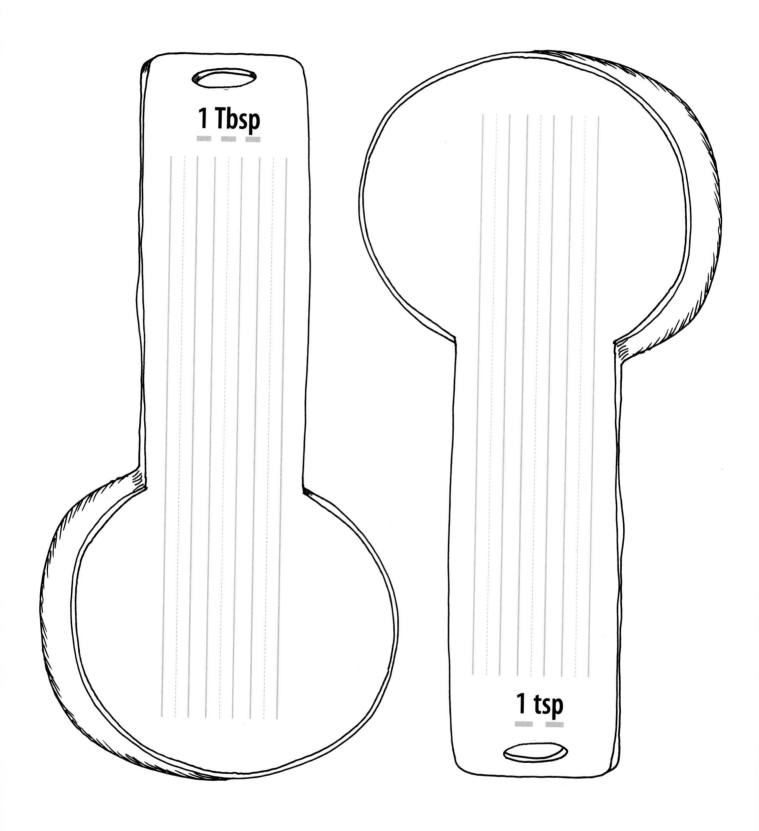

1 Tbsp

1 tsp

9
Cookin' Up Books: Measuring Spoons

1 Cup

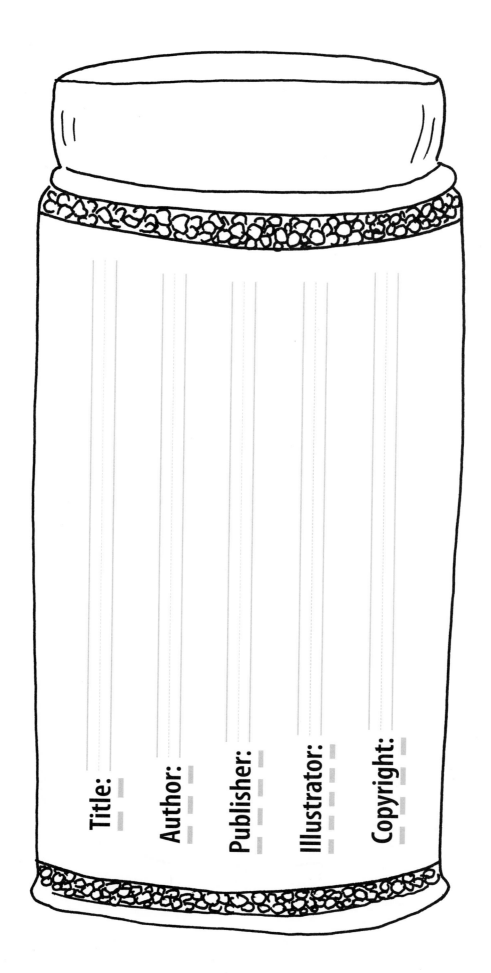

Title:

Author:

Publisher:

Illustrator:

Copyright:

11
Cookin' Up Books: Sprinkles

Read All About It

Grades 3–12

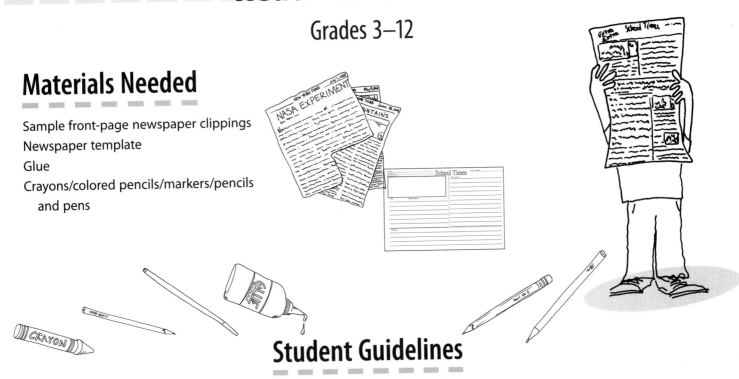

Materials Needed

Sample front-page newspaper clippings
Newspaper template
Glue
Crayons/colored pencils/markers/pencils
and pens

Student Guidelines

1. Using sample front-page newspaper clippings as a guide, students will create a front page of a newspaper to demonstrate their understanding of the book. There should be several sections, all with headlines that depict what that section on the front page will be about.

2. Setting: Students will describe in great detail the setting. Descriptions should include weather, the indoor/outdoor location of the story, and the feeling of the overall story.

3. Characters: This section discusses each of the main characters in detail, including the characters' personalities, appearances, and roles in the story.

4. Plot: This is the main portion of the front page and should have an accompanying illustration in the center of the page. The summary of the plot needs to be conveyed without giving away the story's ending. The illustration needs to reflect the description of the plot and include the story title and author.

5. Turning Point: This section will describe the climax, or turning point, in the story and include a small illustration depicting the scene.

6. Resolution: This section will be the smallest section of the front page but will explain the final outcome of the story.

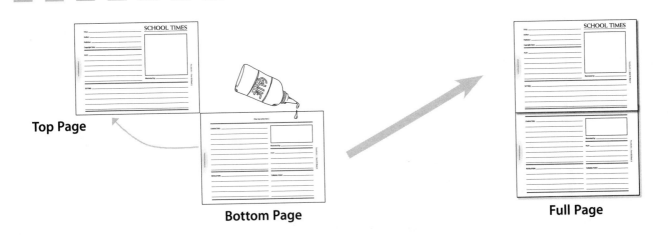

Top Page

Bottom Page

Full Page

SCHOOL TIMES

TITLE: _____

Author: _____

Publisher: _____

Copyright Date: _____

PLOT: _____

_____

_____

_____

_____

_____

Illustrated by: _____

SETTING: _____

_____

_____

(Glue top section here.)

CHARACTERS: _____

Illustrated by: _____

PLOT: _____

TURNING POINT: _____

RESOLUTION: _____

Read All About It (2 of 2)

Bringing Characters to Life
Grades 1–12

Materials Needed

Arm/leg/head templates
11 × 17 white or beige construction paper
Scissors
Crayons/colored pencils/pens

Student Guidelines

- Students will use templates and 11 × 17 sheet of paper to create the main character from the book.
- On the left arm of the character, students will describe the physical characteristics, personality, and role of the main character.
- On the right arm of the character, students will describe the conflict/climax/turning point in the story.
- On the right leg of the character, students will describe the setting and plot of the story.
- On the left leg of the character, students will describe the resolution of the story.
- On the main body of the character, students will illustrate a major scene from the story and include the title, author, illustrator, publisher, and copyright date.
- On the head of the character, students will illustrate the character's face.

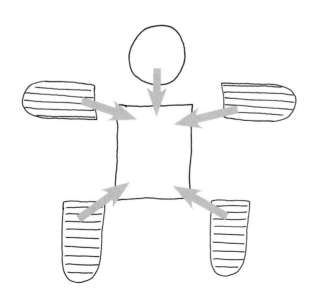

illustration of character's face

13
Head
14
Arms
15
Legs

physical characteristics, personality, and role of main character

conflict/climax/turning point

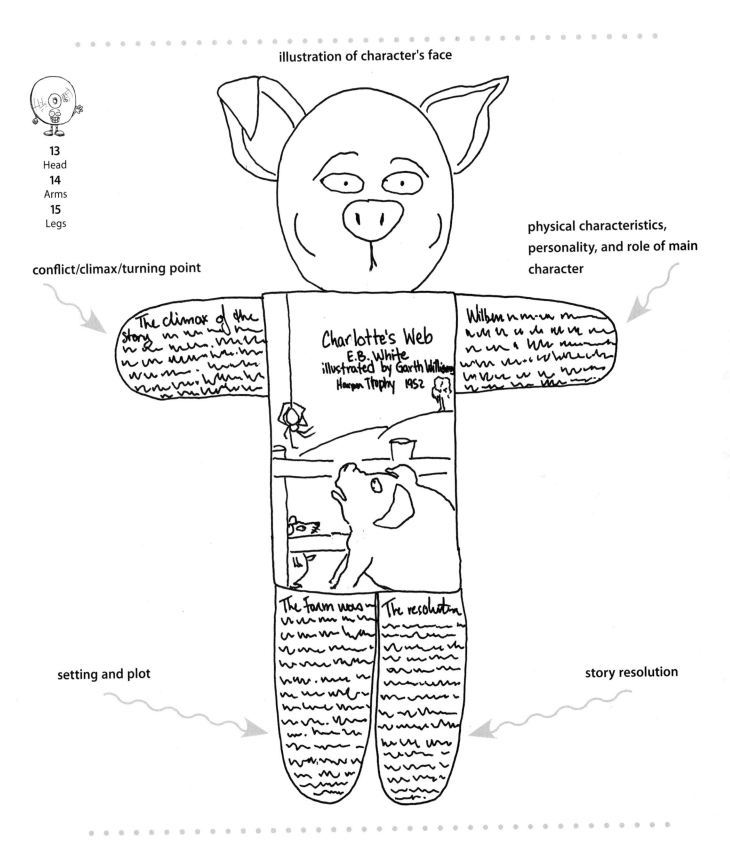

The climax of the story

Wilbur

Charlotte's Web
E.B. White
illustrated by Garth Williams
Harper Trophy 1952

The Farm was

The resolution

setting and plot

story resolution

Letter to the Author
Grades 1–12

Materials Needed

Publishers' addresses
Books whose authors are still alive
Paper and pencil

Student Guidelines

After reading the book, students will write a letter to the author including:

- What was the most interesting scene in the story? Describe it in detail and explain why you liked it.
- Which of the characters do you most closely relate to and why? Use examples from the story to support your reasoning.
- Describe an alternative problem for the story.
- How might you have changed the climax/turning point in the story?
- If you were to rewrite the ending of the story, how would it be written?
- Write a review of the book to accompany your letter.
- Address a regular-size business envelope with the publisher's address and yours.

Depending on the grade level, encourage your students to use more specific details from the story, such as passages and quotations, to support their reasoning. You may even want the students to critically analyze the book for authenticity and cultural sensitivity if it is a book depicting various cultural and/or linguistic struggles, or more traditional books that misrepresent a certain group of people.

Parts of a Friendly Letter

Date
Greeting
Body
Closing
Signature

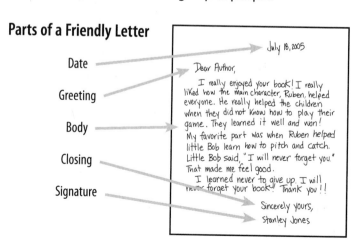

July 18, 2005

Dear Author,

I really enjoyed your book! I really liked how the main character, Ruben, helped everyone. He really helped the children when they did not know how to play their game. They learned it well and won!
My favorite part was when Ruben helped little Bob learn how to pitch and catch. Little Bob said, "I will never forget you." That made me feel good.
I learned never to give up. I will never forget your book! Thank you!!

Sincerely yours,
Stanley Jones

_____,

_____,

Interview a Character

Grades 3–12

Materials Needed

Interview Question Template
Example interview questions
Paper and pencil

Student Guidelines

- After reading the book, students will describe it by using the book summary format to organize their data. Using these responses, students will write the summary of the book as the first page of the Book Report.
- Next, students will formulate 5–10 interview questions written in the third person that they would ask their character. These questions should not be too obvious. They should be more inference related than specific to the book's analysis of the character in question, since the student will have already detailed the character.
- Students will answer their interview questions in the first person as if he or she were the actual character.
- Using the questions and answers, the student will write up the interview in paragraph format as if the interview were to be placed in a magazine. This would include an introduction of the character, the interview itself, and a closing paragraph.
- Students will illustrate a picture of their character to accompany the interview.

Encourage higher level students or students in the upper grades to write their character description in first person as if he or she were the character writing about an interview he or she had engaged in. Then, when writing up the article, the character will come from first person perspective.

Character Interview

Name: _____

Date: _____

1. Describe yourself as if you were one of the characters from the story.

Character Response: _____

_____

_____

2. Explain the problem/conflict you had in the story.

Character Response: _____

_____

_____

3. Explain how you resolved the problem/conflict you had in the story.

Character Response: _____

_____

_____

4. What have you learned from this experience?

Character Response: _____

_____

_____

5. What would you have done differently?

Character Response: _____

_____

_____

On the back of this page, write your favorite quote from the character and include an illustration of your character in your favorite scene.

Character Interview

Name: _____

Date: _____

Develop questions you would want to ask a character from the story.
Answer the questions from the character's point of view/voice.
Draw a picture of the character on the back.

Question/Conversation Starters
Describe · Identify · Why · How · When · Explain · Who · What · Where

1. Question: _____

Character Response: _____

_____

2. Question: _____

Character Response: _____

_____

3. Question: _____

Character Response: _____

_____

4. Question: _____

Character Response: _____

_____

5. Question: _____

Character Response: _____

_____

Social Media Page

Create a social media page about a character/person from a book that you are studying. Include information from the book/his or her life and information that you make up based on your knowledge of the story or the character's life.

Profile

PROFILE PICTURE

_____
Character's Name

PERSONAL INFORMATION

Age: _____   Gender: _____

Birth Date: _____

Relationship Status: _____

OCCUPATION: _____

RELIGION: _____

POLITICAL VIEW: _____

HOMETOWN: _____

EDUCATION

_____

_____

_____

_____

ORGANIZATIONS/GROUPS

_____

_____

_____

_____

FAVORITE QUOTE: _____

_____

FRIENDS

_____
Name

_____
Name

_____
Name

FAVORITES

BOOK: _____

_____

FOOD: _____

_____

HOBBY/INTEREST: _____

_____

SPORT: _____

_____

_____ _____
Name **Post Date**

_____
Caption

_____ _____
Name **Post Date**

_____
Caption

_____ _____
Name **Post Date**

_____
Caption

PEOPLE I ADMIRE

ABOUT ME

CHAT

Social Media Page (2 of 2)

Chirp

Create "chirps" consisting of **no more than 15 words** per chirp that a character from the story would write. These chirps can be about events from the story, how the character is feeling, a conflict in the story, how a conflict was solved, and so forth.

Book Brochure

Grades 4–12

Materials Needed

Sample travel brochures
8½ × 11 white or beige construction paper
Crayons/colored pencils/pens

Student Guidelines

1. Fold the construction paper into three equal parts.

2. Share sample travel brochures as references as well as travel advertisements from the Internet to find important elements often used for travel enticement. Students will describe the setting from their books in great detail on the *inside middle* section of their brochure.

3. On the *inside left flap* of the brochure, students will refer to their books and list the many activities that are available at this place. Students will briefly describe the many activities/events/occurrences that took place in their books.

4. On the *inside right flap* of the brochure, students will refer to their books and describe the type of people who might enjoy the setting. Students will briefly describe the characters from their story as models for people who might visit this setting.

5. On the *back left flap* of the brochure, students will illustrate the setting of their books and list author, illustrator, and publisher.

6. On the *back right flap* of the brochure, students will illustrate a model vacationer by using the main character from their books as the model.

7. On the *back middle* section of the brochure, students will write their name and the copyright date of the book.

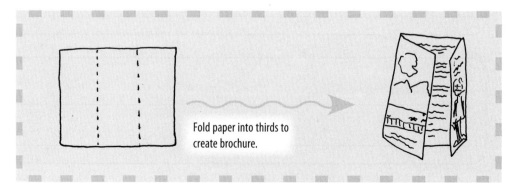

Fold paper into thirds to create brochure.

Inside Left Flap

Activities/Events/Occurrences

List events that took place in the book.

Inside Middle

Setting

Describe with details.

Inside Right Flap

Characters

Describe who would enjoy the setting. Use characters as models of visitors.

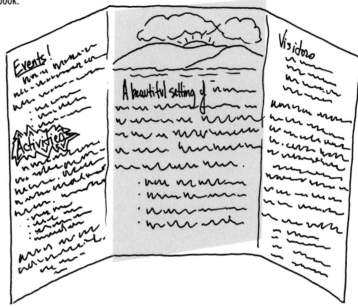

Back Left Flap

Setting
Illustrate.
Include author, illustrator, and publisher.

Back Middle

Student Name
Add copyright date.

Back Right Flap

Main Character
Illustrate main character as model vacationer.

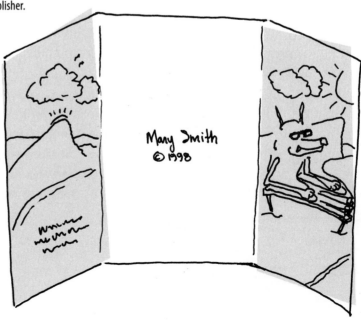

29

Book Report Mobile
Grades 1–12

Materials Needed

Wire or plastic hanger
String
3 × 5 index cards
Colored pencils/crayons/markers/
   pencils and pens

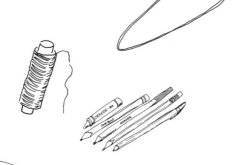

Student Guidelines

Using the index cards, students will write about elements from their books. On one side, students will describe the various elements, and on the other side, students will illustrate the description. The following components must be addressed, one per card:

- Summary of the plot, including the problem, but without giving away the ending
- Description of the setting
- Major turning point in the story, the climax
- The resolution
- Description of the main characters

Once students have written about the story elements and drawn their illustrations, they will attach a string to each of the index cards and then tie the strings to the hanger in the order listed above.

Students who are higher level thinkers or artists may want to draw and cut out characters from the story and describe the characters' traits on the back.

Hints

- Tie cards at different lengths.
- Cut each card into a different geometric shape/form.

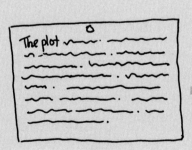

FRONT

- Summary—plot/problem
- Setting—detailed description
- Climax—major turning point
- Resolution
- Main characters

BACK

Descriptive Diary
Grades 2–12

Materials Needed

Sample diary entry templates
Light colored 8½ × 11 sheets
   of construction paper
Brads
Crayons/colored pencils/markers/
   pencils and pens

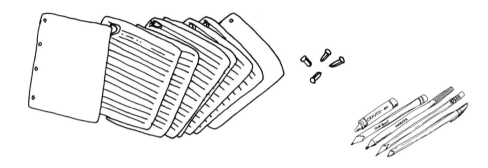

plot

problem

setting

climax

Student Guidelines

Using the diary entry templates or something similar, students will create six diary entries, each focusing on a particular element from the story. The following components must be addressed in first person:

- *Summary of the **plot***: Dear Diary: Today we went to Mrs. Pandeski's house. She told us the story of how she met Mr. Pandeski right after the war. I figure he was lucky to live after what he went through. . . .

- ***Problem** without giving away the ending*: Dear Diary: When I got home from Mrs. Pandeski's house, I got to thinking about what an adventure Mr. Pandeski had while fighting the war. I can't believe she wouldn't want him to be honored at the reception even though he has now passed away. . . .

- *Detailed description of the **setting***: Dear Diary: Mr. Pandeski's life during the war was nothing like I had ever heard about before. He had to sleep on the ground most nights. Even when he went back to the barracks after being in the field for several days, it was not like home. . . .

- *Major turning point in the story, the **climax***: Dear Diary: Mrs. Pandeski's son called today while I was visiting. He was upset with Mrs. Pandeski because she didn't want to go to the reception to honor Mr. Pandeski. The memories are just too much for her. . . .

resolution

main
characters

- ***Resolution*** *in the story*: Dear Diary: Mrs. Pandeski finally decided to go to the reception so long as her son accompanied her. She didn't want to go alone. In fact, she invited me and I went, too. . . .

- *Description of **main characters***: Dear Diary: Mrs. Pandeski is the most wonderful woman. . . .

Compile the diary entries and place them between two 8½ × 11 sheets of construction paper. Use the brads to secure the diary entries and construction paper. Illustrate the main idea of the story on the front cover and add title, author, illustrator, and publisher.

Day: _____

Date: _____

Dear Diary: _____

_____
_____
_____
_____
_____
_____
_____
_____
_____
_____
_____
_____
_____
_____
_____
_____
_____
_____
_____
_____
_____
_____
_____
_____
_____
_____
_____
_____
_____

Character Puppet
Grades K–6

Materials Needed

White or brown lunch bag
Crayons/colored pencils/markers
Scissors
Glue
Yarn in a variety of colors
Construction paper in various
   shades of brown

Student Guidelines

1. On the inside of the lunch bag, students will write their own names.
2. On the back of the lunch bag, students will describe in detail the main character. They will include physical traits, personality, and role of the character in the story. Students will include quotations or passages from the story that depicts the main character's role in the plot.
3. On the front of the lunch bag where the flap naturally folds, students will describe in detail the main character of their book. This will include the plot of the story, setting of the story, problem in the story, climax of the story, and resolution of the story.
4. Under the flap of the lunch bag, students will write the title, author, illustrator if applicable, the publisher, and the copyright date.
5. Using the construction paper, glue, scissors, yarn, and crayons/pencils/markers, students will create a character puppet. They may want to use the construction paper to draw and cut out a face. The yarn can be used as hair. Additional construction paper can be used to make arms, legs, feet, clothes, and so forth.

Extension Ideas

- **Puppet Interviews.** Students can have puppet interviews with other students. One student would ask questions while the other would answer them in the character of his or her puppet.
- **Writing Dialogue.** Students can partner up and one student can deliver dialogue using his or her puppet, while the other student practices writing down the dialogue in conversation form.
- **Strange Stories.** Students can pair up and use their puppets to have a conversation with another character from a different story; both students stay in character and create new dialogue.
- **Class Performances.** Several students reading the same book may choose to create many of the characters from the same book and perform a scene from the book for the class.

Traditional Book Report Format
Grades 1–12

Materials Needed

Book report elements:

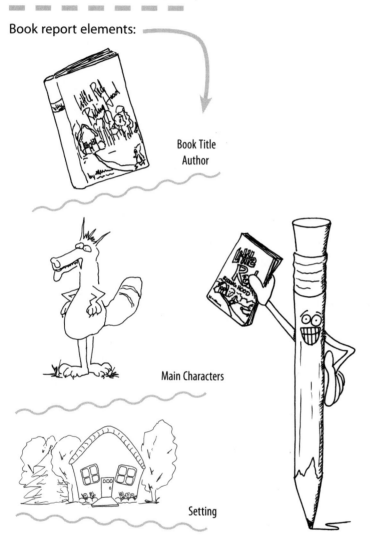

Book Title
Author

Main Characters

Setting

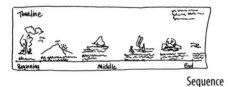

Sequence

Scenes

Student Guidelines

Students will include the following elements in their book report description. This is an outline for the students to collect information before writing their book report in paragraph form:

I. Main Characters
   A. Name and Brief Description
   B. Name and Brief Description
   C. Name and Brief Description

II. Detailed Description of the Setting

III. Summary of the Plot in Appropriate Sequence

IV. Favorite Two to Five Scenes in the Book
   A. Describe in Detail
   B. Describe in Detail
   C. Describe in Detail
   D. Describe in Detail
   E. Describe in Detail

V. Criticism of the Book
   A. Would You Recommend?
   B. Why or Why Not?

VI. Overall Opinion of the Book
   A. Example Supporting Rationale
   B. Example Supporting Rationale
   C. Example Supporting Rationale

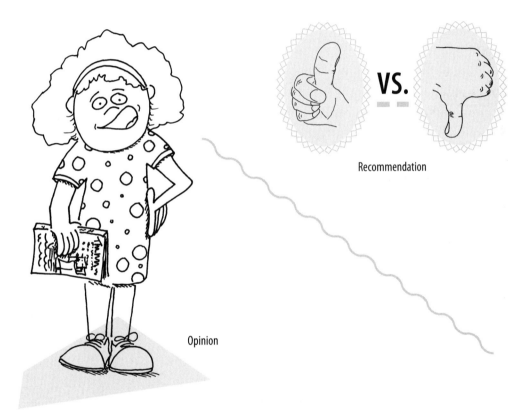

VS.

Recommendation

Opinion

Use grade-level appropriate book report formats.

• • • • • • •

The depth of opinion and number of supporting rationales will vary with grade/ability levels.

Book Report

Directions

- Read book.
- Write book report.
- Illustrate your favorite part.

Name: _____

Date: _____

Title: _____

Author: _____

Illustrator: _____

1. Write three sentences telling what the book is about.

_____

_____

_____

_____

_____

_____

_____

_____

_____

_____

_____

2. What was your favorite part (three or more sentences)?

_____

_____

_____

_____

_____

_____

_____

_____

_____

_____

_____

_____

3. Draw a picture about the story (on the back). Include characters and setting.

Book Report

Name: _____

Date: _____

Book Information

Title: _____

Author: _____

Illustrator: _____

Copyright date: _____

Number of pages: _____

Genre: ☐ Fiction ☐ Nonfiction ☐ Fable
      ☐ Fantasy ☐ Fairy tale ☐ Expository
      ☐ Biography ☐ Autobiography

Book Report Outline

Select an outline for your book report.

1. a. State subject.
   b. List three facts you learned.
   c. Describe the most interesting part.
2. Describe:
   a. the main characters
   b. the setting
   c. the conflict/problem
   d. the resolution
   e. personal connection/opinion

_____

_____

_____

_____

_____

_____

_____

_____

_____

_____

_____

_____

_____

_____

_____

_____

Draw a picture on the back of your favorite part of the story.

Additional Ideas for Responding to Literature

Grades K–12

1. **Comic Strip.** Draw a comic strip of your favorite scene or of the main idea of the story. Fold an 11" × 14" piece of white construction paper in half. Cut down the middle. (One sheet is enough for two students.) Fold like an accordion, and develop a comic strip based on the story.

2. **Diorama.** Use a shoebox or similar item to make a model of a scene or the main idea of the story.

3. **Résumé.** Using what you know about one of the main characters from a story, create a résumé based on his or her personal characteristics.

4. **Mini-book.** Create a mini-book about the story by either sequencing the plot or describing each of the characters.

5. **Friendly Letter.** Write a letter to one of the characters you most closely relate to from your story.

6. **Movie Poster.** Make a poster about your book as if you were introducing it to the world like a movie.

7. **Character Tree.** Make a character tree illustrating the characters on the tree branches with a short description of each character's role in the book.

8. **Postcard.** Create a postcard that you would like to send to one of the characters from the story. In it, recall the events he or she was involved in within the story and why you would like to meet the character in real life.

9. **Dear Abby.** Write a "Dear Abby" letter about a problem you are having as one of the characters in the story. You can exchange these with classmates, and you will respond to their problems.

10. **Timeline.** Create a timeline sequencing the events in the story. Above each entry into the timeline, illustrate the event.

11. **Crystal Ball.** Predict the future for the main character/s in the story. For example, Little Red Riding Hood: what do you think happens to her in the future?

12. **Want Ad.** Write an ad for one of the characters as if he or she were looking for a friend. Draw upon the character's traits to describe his or her persona.

13. **Obituary.** Write an obituary for one of the characters. Include lifetime accomplishments using scenes from the book to describe him or her.

14. **Bookmark.** Make a bookmark addressing key elements of a book report such as plot, summary, setting, conflict, and resolution on one side. Illustrate a scene from the book on the other.

15. **Empty the Trash.** Fill in the trashcan with illustrations and words to describe what would be found in one of the character's trash.

Name: _____ Date: _____

Create a résumé for a character in the book. Include facts or create details based on what you know about the character. Select information with a job goal or professional objective in mind.

RÉSUMÉ

_____
Full Name

Contact Information: Address _____

Phone _____

E-mail _____

Professional Objective: State goal. _____

_____

Education: List in chronological order, starting with most recent.

_____

_____

_____

Work History: List in chronological order, starting with most recent.

_____

_____

_____

Professional Experience: List in chronological order, starting with most recent.

_____

_____

_____

Interests: List interests or hobbies that demonstrate unique characteristics about yourself.

_____

_____

_____

Dear Abby Book Report

Name: _____ Date: _____

Write a "Dear Abby" letter from a character's point of view, seeking advice for a problem in the story. Write a second letter from "Dear Abby" that gives advice to the character.

_____
Date

Dear Abby,

_____

_____

_____

_____

_____

_____

_____

_____

_____ ,
                                    Creative Closing

_____
Character's Name

_____
Date

Dear _____ ,
      Character's Name

_____

_____

_____

_____

_____

_____

_____

_____

Good luck,
Abby

Crystal Ball Book Report

Name: _____ Date: _____

Predict the future for a character by drawing items that you would find in the character's future. Write a brief explanation on a separate sheet of paper, explaining why you included the items that you did.

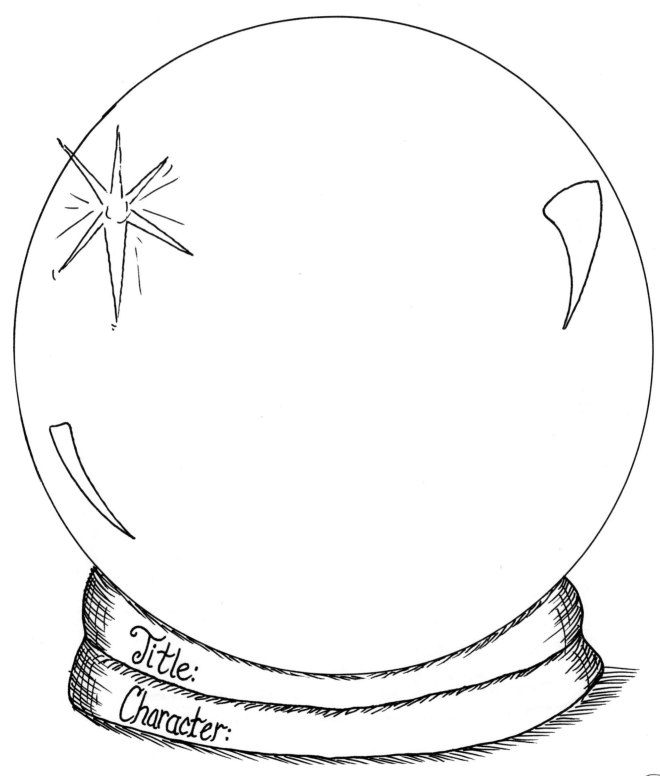

Title:

Character:

Name: _____   Date: _____

On a separate piece of paper, create a wanted poster for a character in the story that is part of the problem/conflict. Explain in detail why the character is wanted.

Write an obituary for a character in the story. Be sure to include the character's bio, whom he or she is survived by, accomplishments in the story, brief timeline or history from the story, and details on the character's memorial.

OBITUARY

R.I.P.

_____
Character's Full Name

_____ – _____

_____

_____

_____

_____

_____

_____

_____

_____

_____

_____

_____

_____

_____

_____

_____

_____

_____

_____

_____

_____

_____

_____

_____

Bookmark

Create a bookmark for a story you have read. On the front, draw your favorite scene and write the title and author. On the back, write about the various components of the story. Cut out, fold, and tape.

_____
Title

_____
Author

_____
Illustrator

_____
Main Character/s

Summary: _____

_____

_____

_____

_____

_____

_____

_____

_____

Why: _____

_____

_____

_____

☐ Recommend   ☐ Don't recommend

Name: _____   Date: _____

Empty the Trash

Draw or make a collage featuring several items that would be found in the main character's trash. Write a sentence explaining why those items would be found in his or her trash.

Math

This chapter has been designed to offer creative ways to teach math using hands-on approaches that are meaningful, fun, and engaging. Tools include 10 grids, clock templates, fraction templates, tangrams, pentominoes, 3-D geometric patterns/shapes templates, and the like. Teach geometry skills using the shapes, forms, geometric formulas, and dot to dot templates. Designed to provide hands-on math experiences and practical applications, this chapter is full of support pages for math fundamentals, from blank calendars and number charts to daily math review sheets, a multiplication table, flash cards, and money manipulative pages.

These strategies and activities are tools that relate to teaching from the Common Core Standards for Math (http://www.corestandards.org/math). These standards define what students should understand and be able to do in their study of mathematics. The standards are grade-level specific, but all begin with the following general standards for Mathematical Practice for all teachers to consider when planning grade-level mathematics curriculum:

1. Make sense of problems and persevere in solving them
2. Reason abstractly and quantitatively
3. Construct viable arguments, and critique the reasoning of others
4. Model with mathematics
5. Use appropriate tools strategically
6. Attend to precision
7. Look for and make use of structure
8. Look for and express regularity in repeated reasoning

Tangrams

According to "Randy" at the Tangram website, http://tangrams.ca/inner/tanhist.htm, the invention of the tangram puzzle is unrecorded in history. The earliest known Chinese book is dated 1813, but the puzzle was very old by then. One reason for this lack of historical information could be that at that time in China, its country of origin, it was originally considered a game for women and children. This would have made it unworthy of "serious" study and unlikely to be written about.

Because tangrams are simple, these puzzles are accessible to many people. A classic puzzle, tangrams appeal to young and old, the serious and the carefree. Mathematicians are often interested in them because of the geometry and ratios of the pieces. They are also used in classrooms around the world to teach basic math ideas in an interesting way.

"The Chinese Puzzle" encouraged many books and picture card sets. Some of the more elaborate tangram pieces are carved from and/or inlaid with ivory, jade, and other fine materials. Less expensive pieces are made from wood or fired clay. Today, pieces can easily be purchased and are often made of plastic. Some teachers use card stock to photocopy the pieces and then laminate them so every student can make his or her own set, as we recommend you do. Use our template to make one set for yourself and each of your students.

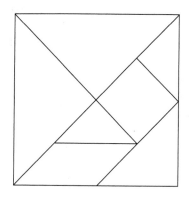

Again, according to Randy's Tangram website, the four classic rules are: you must use all seven tans, they must lie flat, they must touch, and none may overlap.

The following books about tangrams might be helpful to you and your students:

Campbell-Ernst, L. (2005). *Tangram Magician*. Handprint Books. ISBN 1593541066.

Hale, H. (1997). *Tangrams*. Tarquin Publications, UK. ISBN 0906212561.

Maccarone, G., & Burns, M. (1997). *Three Pigs, One Wolf, and Seven Magic Shapes*. Scholastic, Inc. ISBN 0590308572.

Marsh, V., & Luzadder, P. (1996). *Story Puzzles: Tales in the Tangram Tradition*. Highsmith Press, LLC. ISBN 0917846591.

Tompert, A. (1997). *Grandfather Tang's Story*. Bantam Doubleday Dell Books for Young Readers. ISBN 0517885581.

Tangrams

Color and cut out to create your own tangrams.

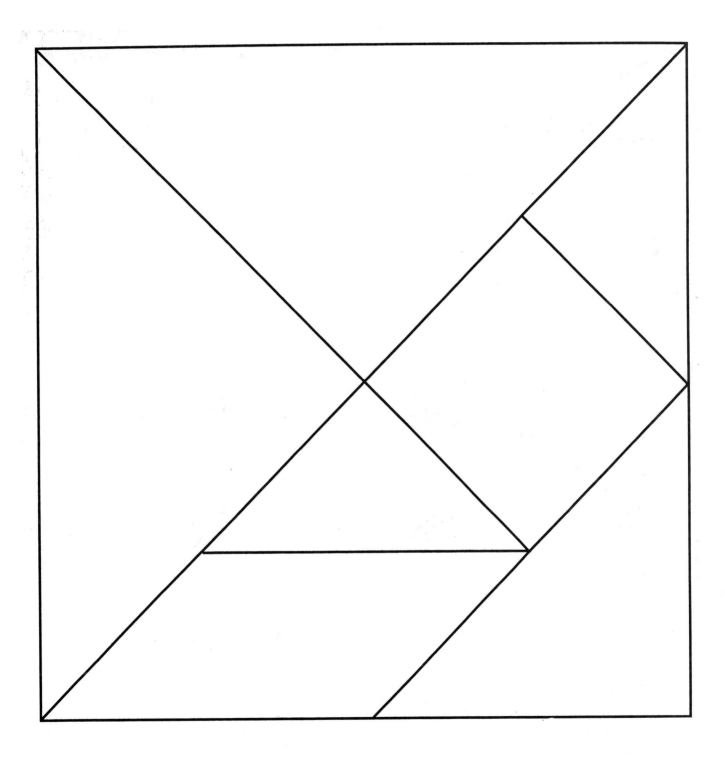

Solid Geometry: Three-Dimensional Objects

It is important for students to have the opportunity to study the geometric properties of three-dimensional objects so they can explore their world in the geometric sense. Models are very important, and if wooden or plastic solids are not available, you may choose to have each student make his or her own model for the various geometric objects displayed in this section.

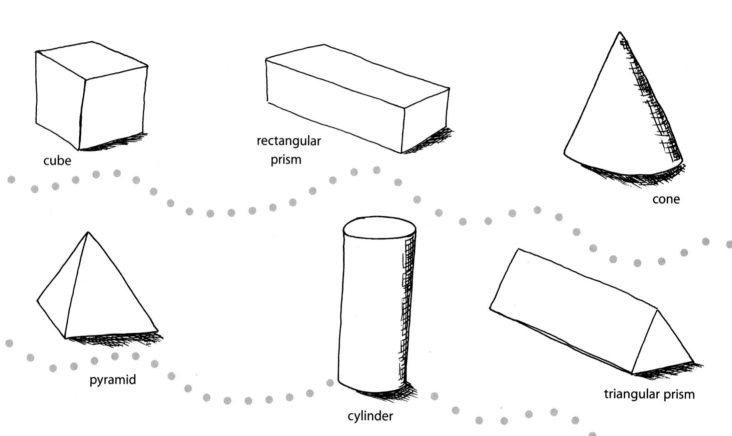

cube

rectangular
prism

cone

pyramid

cylinder

triangular prism

These books about solid geometry and three-dimensional objects might be helpful to you and your students:

Dodds, D. (1996). *Shape of Things.* Candlewick Press. ISBN 1564026981.

Fitzgibbon, K. (1999). *Geometry for Primary Grades.* Steck-Vaughn Publishers. ISBN 0817258078.

Math Forum. (2004). *Dr. Math Introduces Geometry: Learning Geometry Is Easy! Just Ask Dr. Math.* Wiley, John & Sons, Inc. ISBN 0471225541.

Neuschwander, C. (2005). *Mummy Math: An Adventure in Geometry.* Holt Henry Books for Young Readers. ISBN 0805075054.

Smith, A. (1990). *Cut and Assemble 3-D Geometric Shapes.* Dover Publications. ISBN 0486250938.

Cube

Fold along lines and glue tabs.

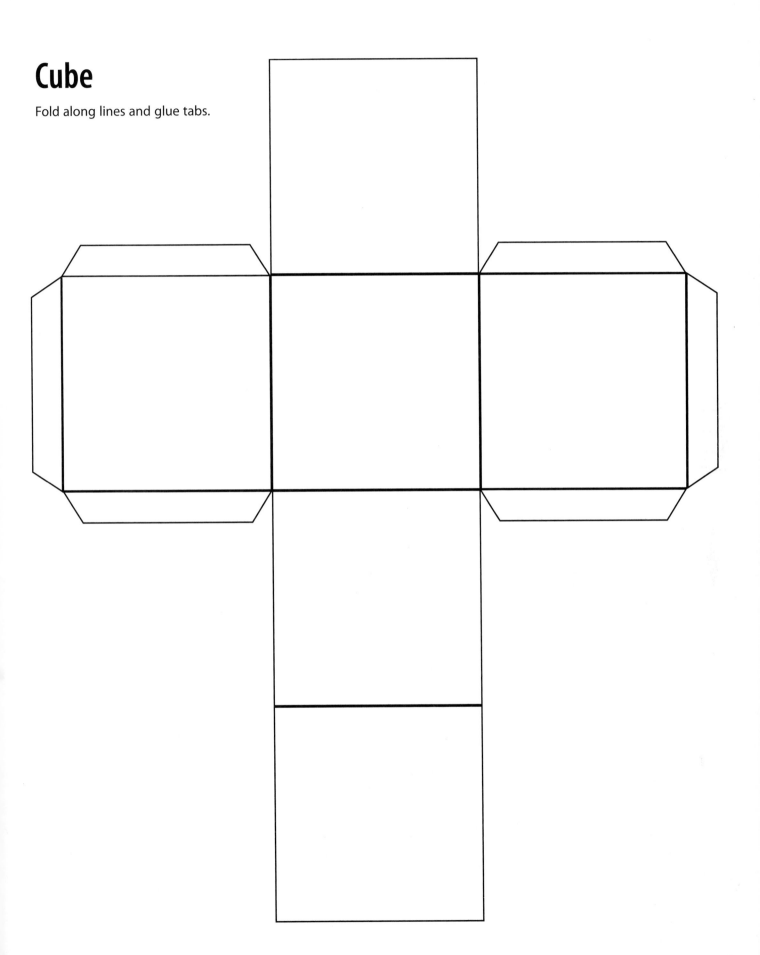

Rectangular Prism

Fold along lines and glue tabs.

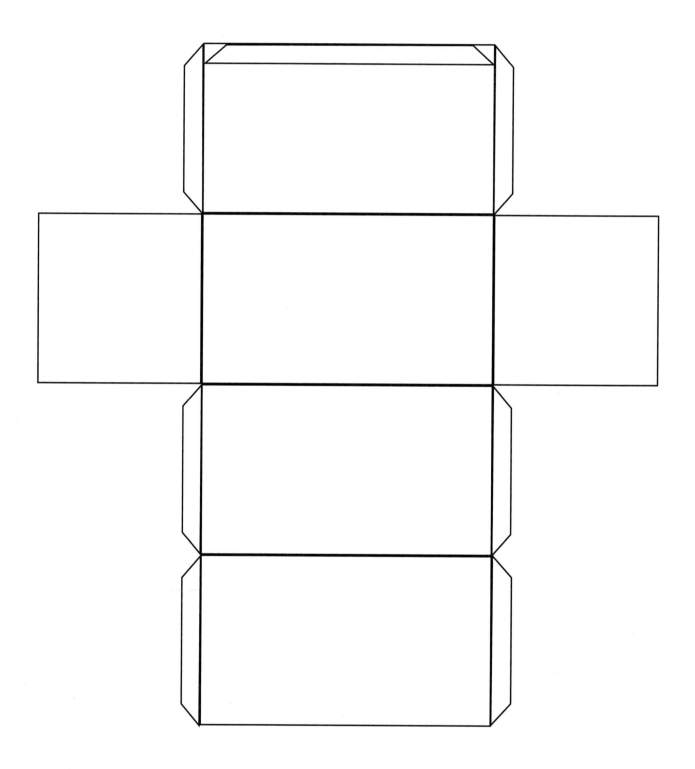

Triangular Prism

Fold along lines and glue tabs.

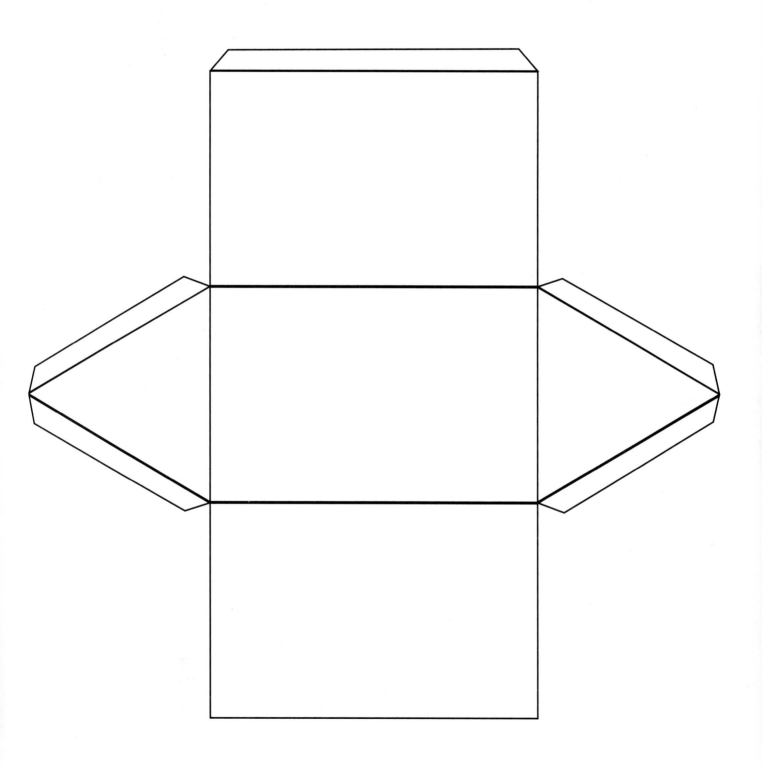

Triangular Pyramid

Fold along lines and glue tabs.

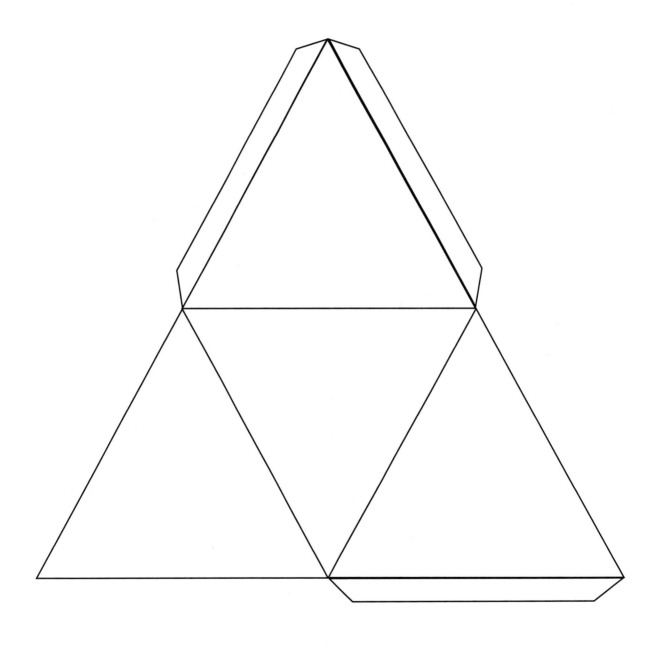

Solid Geometry:
Three-Dimensional Objects

Cylinder

Fold along lines and glue tabs.

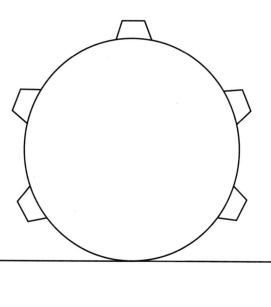

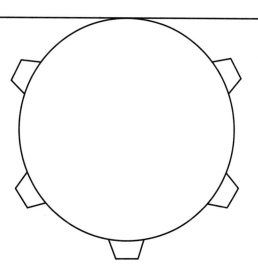

Cone

Fold along lines and glue tabs.

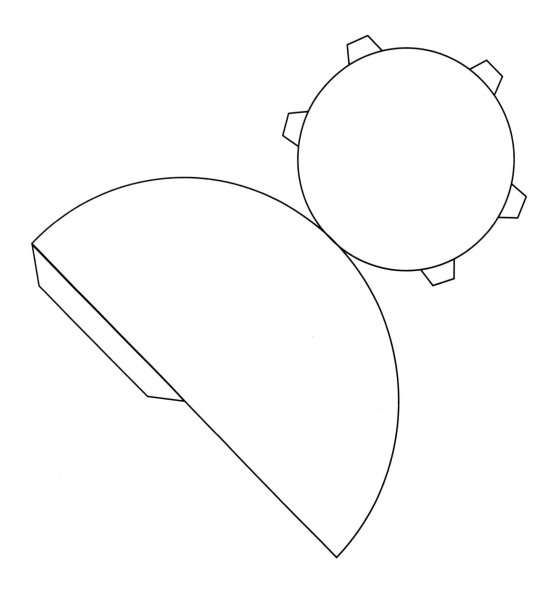

Shapes

Color and write the name of each shape.

square

rectangle

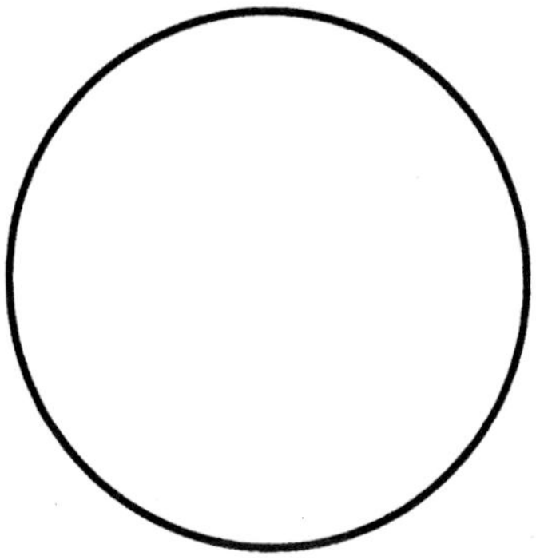

circle

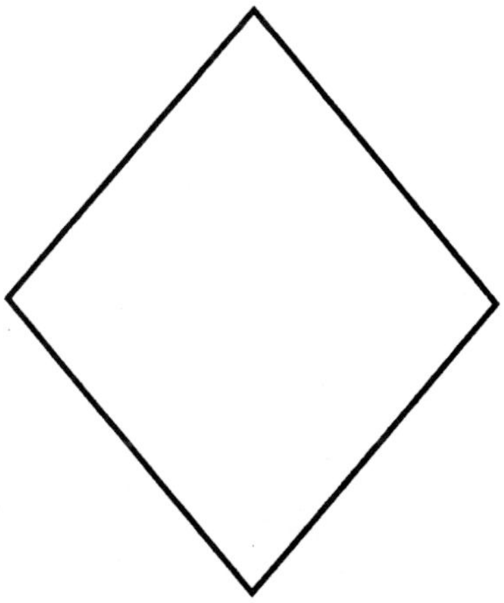

diamond

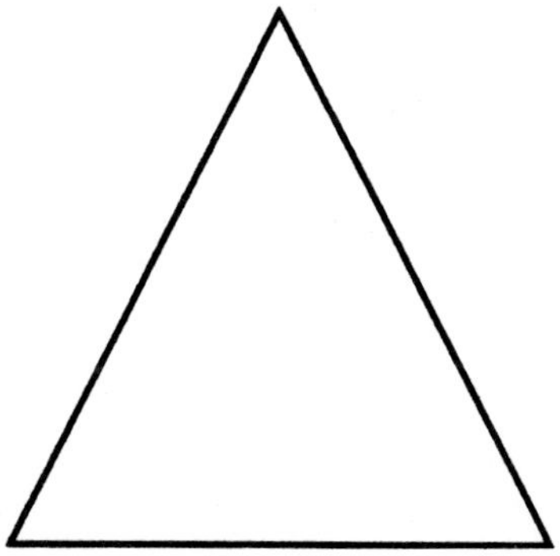

triangle

Shapes

Write the name of each shape.

Name: _____

Name: _____

Sides: _____

Vertices: _____

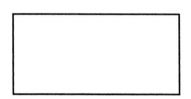

Name: _____

Sides: _____

Vertices: _____

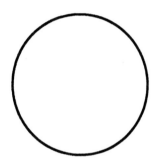

Name: _____

Sides: _____

Vertices: _____

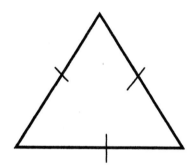

Name: _____

Sides: _____

Vertices: _____

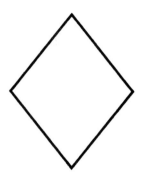

Name: _____

Sides: _____

Vertices: _____

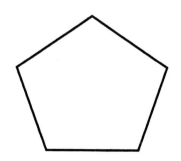

Name: _____

Sides: _____

Vertices: _____

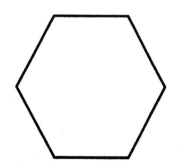

Name: _____

Sides: _____

Vertices: _____

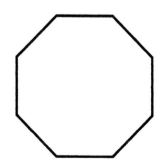

Name: _____

Sides: _____

Vertices: _____

Name:

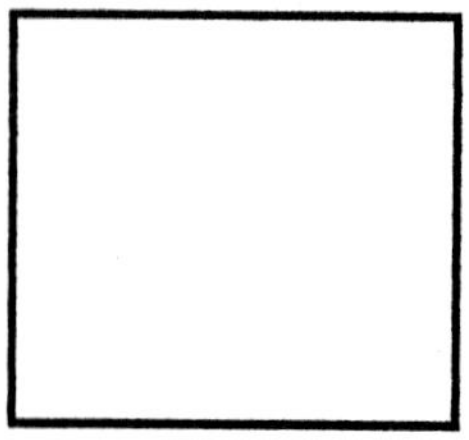

Square

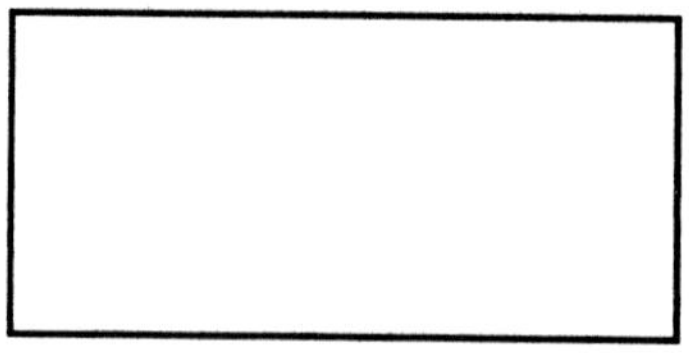

Rectangle

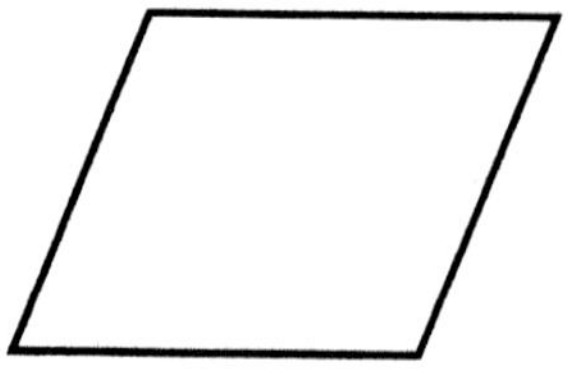

Rhombus

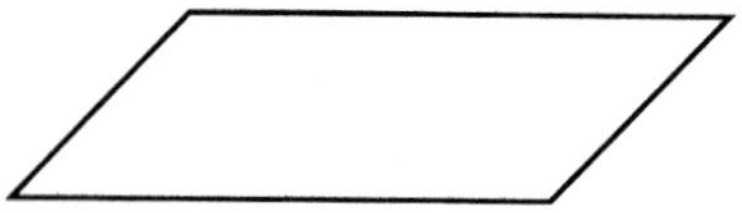

Parallelogram

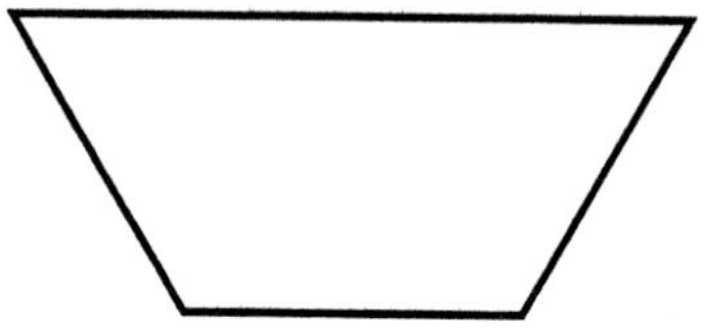

Trapezoid

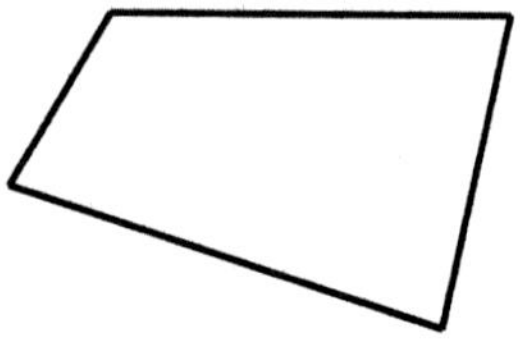

Quadrilateral

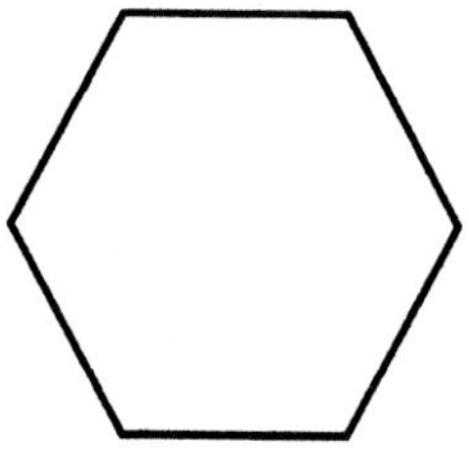

Hexagon

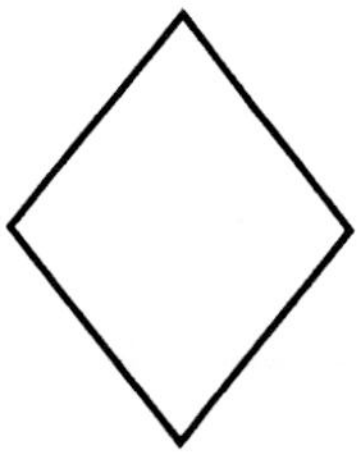

Diamond

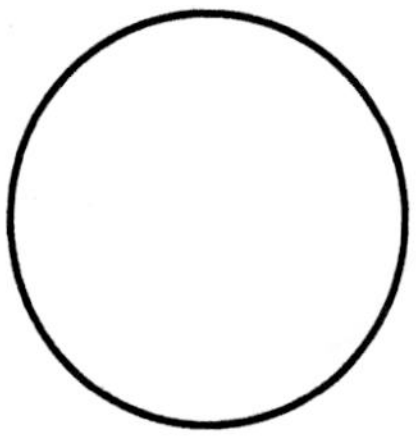

Circle

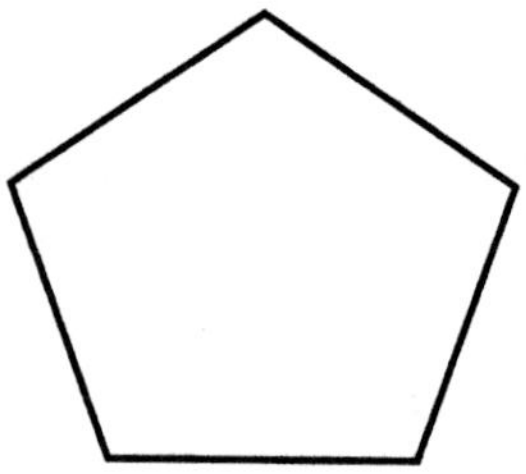

Pentagon

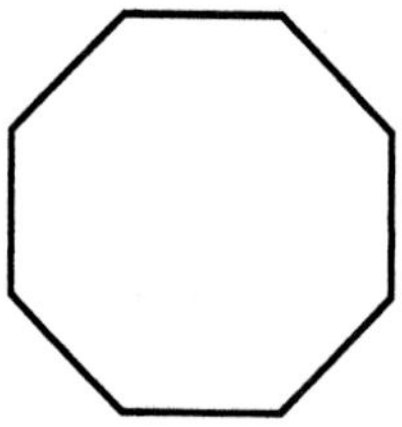

Octagon

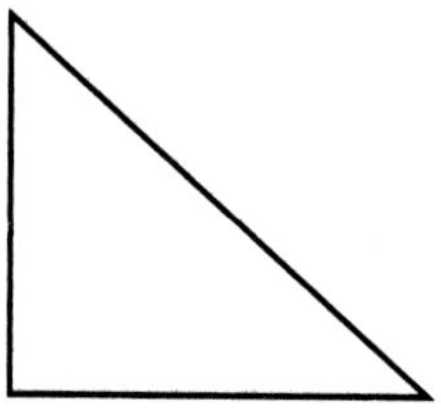

Right Triangle

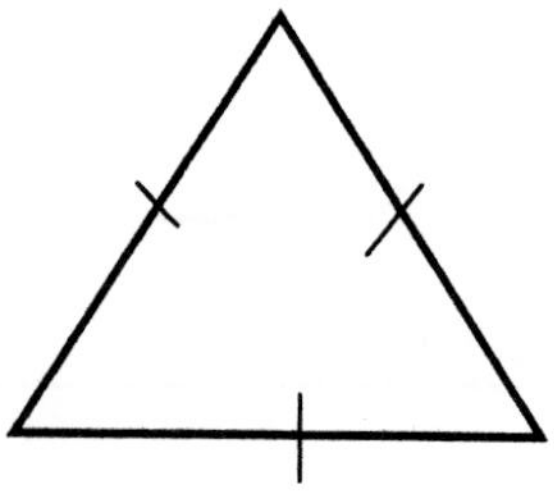

Equilateral Triangle

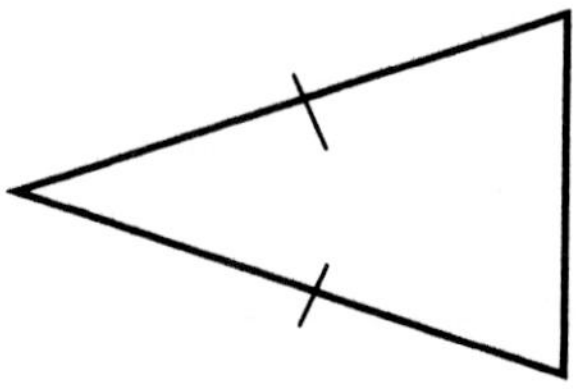

Isosceles Triangle

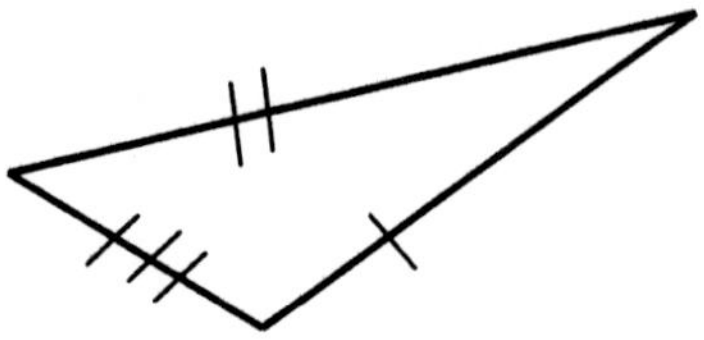

Scalene Triangle

Forms

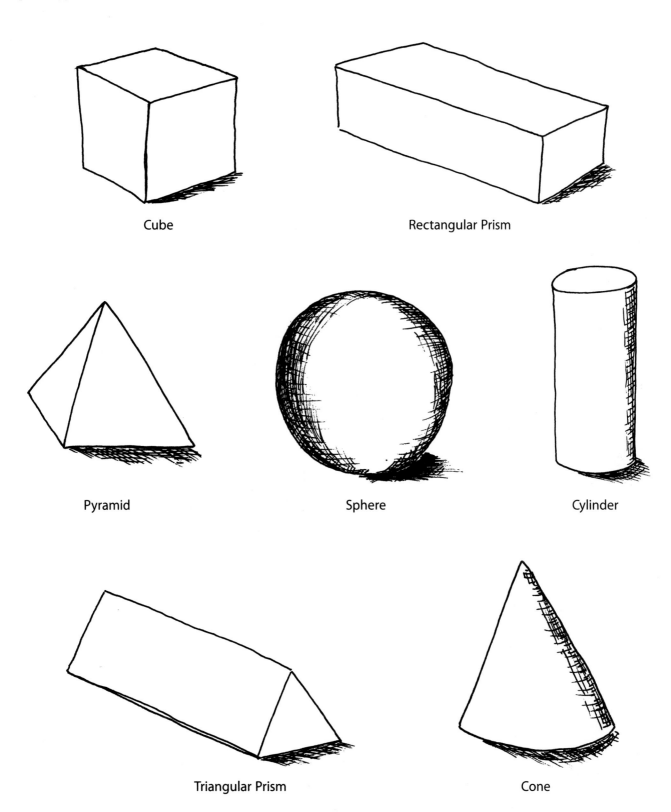

Cube

Rectangular Prism

Pyramid

Sphere

Cylinder

Triangular Prism

Cone

Name: _____

Forms

Write the name of each form.

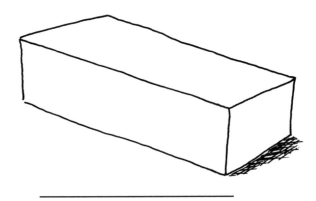

_____

_____

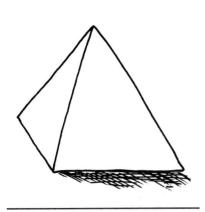

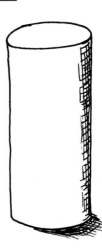

_____

_____

_____

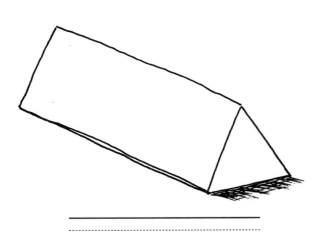

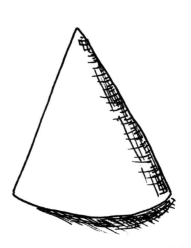

_____

_____

43
Forms 2

Name: _____

Forms

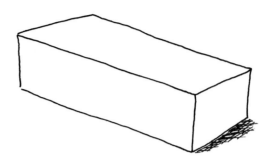

Name: _____

Faces: _____

Corners: _____

Edges: _____

Name: _____

Faces: _____

Corners: _____

Edges: _____

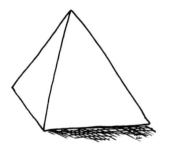

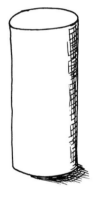

Name: _____

Faces: _____

Corners: _____

Edges: _____

Name: _____

Faces: _____

Corners: _____

Edges: _____

Name: _____

Faces: _____

Corners: _____

Edges: _____

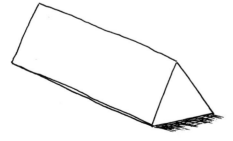

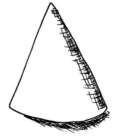

Name: _____

Faces: _____

Corners: _____

Edges: _____

Name: _____

Faces: _____

Corners: _____

Edges: _____

Geometric Formulas

P = perimeter   l = length π = 3.14
A = area   w = width   C = circumference
V = volume   b = base   r = radius
s = side   h = height   d = diameter

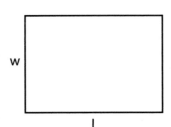

Square
P = s + s + s + s
$A = s^2$

Rectangle
P = 2l + 2w
A = l × w

Parallelogram
P = s + s + s + s
A = b × h

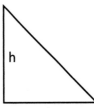

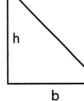

Triangle
P = s + s + s
A = ½bh

Circle
C = 2πr
$A = \pi r^2$

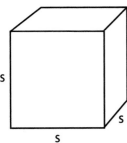

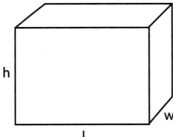

Cube
$V = s^3$

Rectangular Prism
V = l × w × h

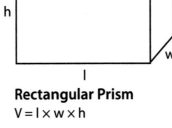

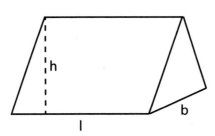

Cylinder
$V = (\pi r^2)h$

Triangular Prism
V = ½bhl

Name: _____

Date: _____

Connect the dots to create shapes.

Dominoes

This is a game played by two or more people. It requires 28 small rectangular blocks sometimes made of ivory, wood, or plastic. The game appeared first in China in the fourteenth century. The first recorded reference in Europe is from Italy where dominoes were played in the courts of Venice and Naples. Although domino tiles are clearly of Chinese inheritance, there is debate over whether the game played by Europeans was brought by the Chinese to Europe in the eighteenth century or, in fact, was invented independently. European dominoes are shorter than Chinese ones. There is a single tile for each variation of the throw of two dice or a blank, making a total of 28 tiles. This is the standard or "double-six" set and, as in China, various games can be played with it. Double-twelve sets (91 tiles) are popular in America, and double-nine sets (55 tiles) also exist. Today, dominoes or variants of it are played in almost all countries of the world, but it is most popular in Latin America. More information about dominoes can be found at the website tradgames.org.uk/games/Dominoes.htm.

Dominoes are numbered in pairs. Each domino has a paired combination of the numbers 0–6. The following is a breakdown of those combinations:

Dominoes

0–0						
0–1	1–1					
0–2	1–2	2–2				
0–3	1–3	2–3	3–3			
0–4	1–4	2–4	3–4	4–4		
0–5	1–5	2–5	3–5	4–5	5–5	
0–6	1–6	2–6	3–6	4–6	5–6	6–6

(Example: 4–3)

The following books about dominoes might interest you and your students:

Jaffe, E., Labbo, L., & Field, S. (2002). *Dominoes: Games Around the World*. Compass Point Books. ISBN 0756501326.

Kelley, J., & Lugo, M. (2003). *The Little Giant Book of Dominoes*. Sterling Publishing Company, Inc. ISBN 1402702906.

Lankford, M., & Dugan, K. (1998). *Dominoes Around the World*. William Morrow and Company, Inc. ISBN 0688140513.

Long, L. (1996). *Domino Addition*. Charlesbridge Publishing, Inc. ISBN 0881068772.

Oringel, S., & Silverman, H. (1997). *Math Activities with Dominoes*. ETA/Cuisenaire. ISBN 157452027X.

Playing Dominoes

Student Instructions

Simply playing dominoes:

- Place all dominoes facedown on the table. (You can draw dominoes to establish player order.)
- Each player selects four dominoes.
- The lead player places a double down on the table (if possible, not necessary).
- The next player lays down a domino that matches either end of the first. If player has no match, that player selects another domino and skips his or her turn.
- A player wins when all of his or her dominoes are used.
- If no one can continue play, then the player with the fewest dominoes left wins.

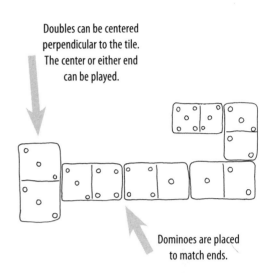

Doubles can be centered perpendicular to the tile. The center or either end can be played.

Dominoes are placed to match ends.

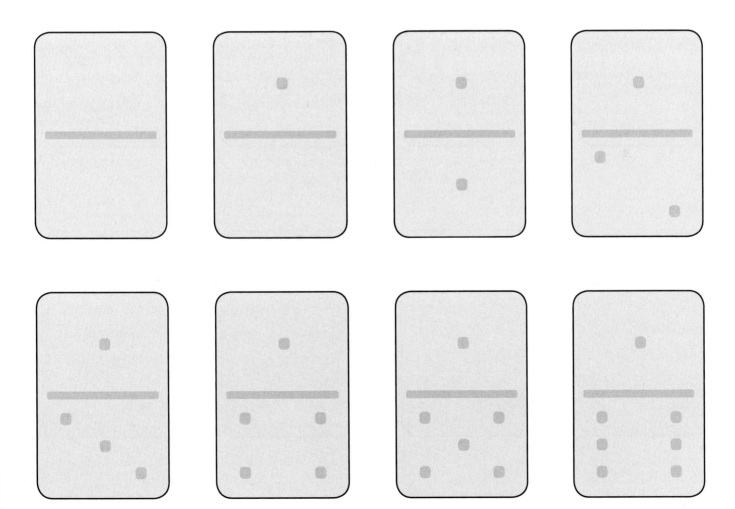

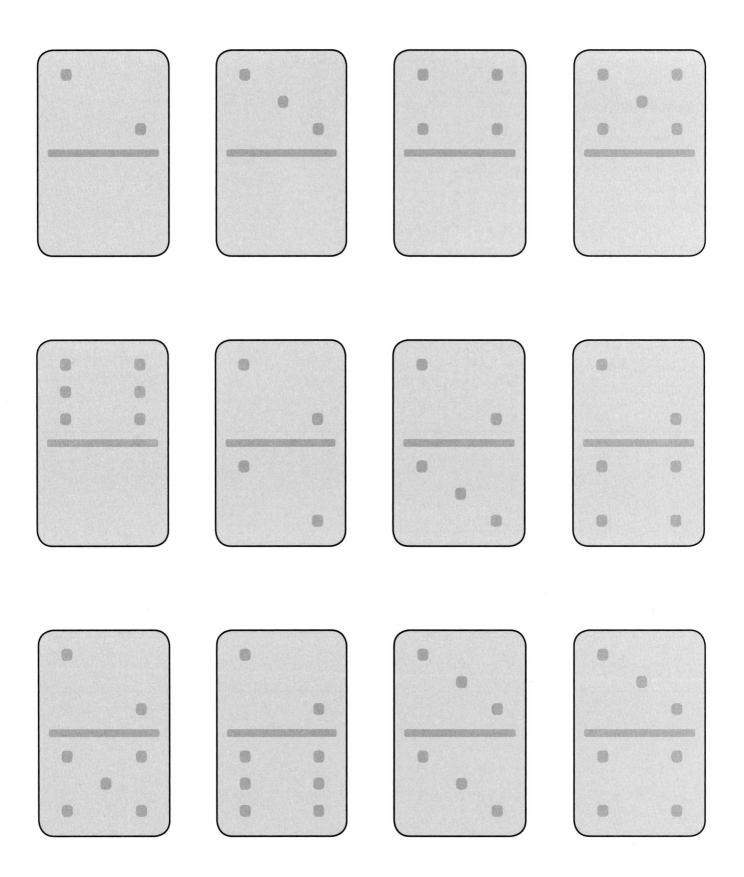

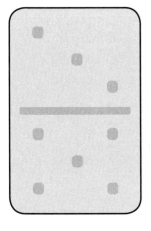
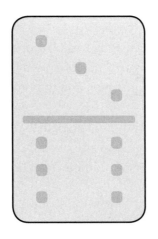
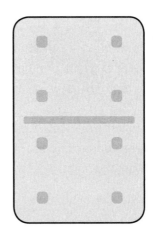
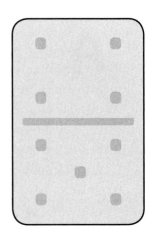

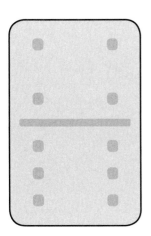
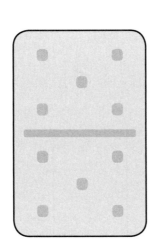
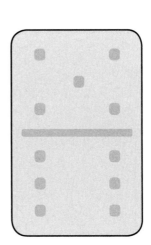
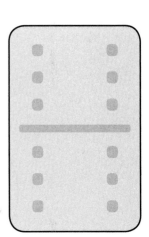

Domino Fun!

- Decorate your dominoes with a theme.
- Play dominoes.
- Draw dominoes and +, −, or × the two numbers on the domino piece.
- Select a set number of dominoes to + up.
- Look up other variations of domino games on the Internet.
- Create your own domino game.

Fractions

A fraction is a part of a whole or a part of a group, such as one-half (½), one-third (⅓), two-thirds (⅔), or one-quarter (¼). For example, one-half of a pie is a fraction of a pie. A fraction can be expressed in the form ᵃ/b, where the top number, *a*, is called the numerator, and the bottom number, *b*, is called the denominator.

The following pages contain a pizza, a pie, and a candy bar template that can be used by students to practice dividing wholes into fractions. Shape templates have also been provided for additional practice. Fractions can be assigned, and a fraction bulletin board can be created and used as a reference while studying fractions.

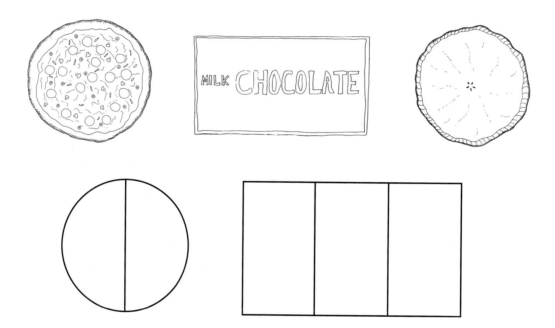

The following list includes books that are wonderful to use in getting your students excited about learning fractions. In addition, you will find fraction templates in this book that you may choose to copy onto colorful card stock, laminate, and have students cut out to create their own fraction kits.

Adler, D. (1996). *Fraction Fun*. Holiday House, Inc. ISBN 0823412598.

Dobson, C. (2003). *Pizza Counting Book*. Charlesbridge Publishing, Inc. ISBN 0881063398.

Pallotta, J. (2003). *Apple Fractions*. Scholastic, Inc. ISBN 043989011.

Pallotta, J., & Bolster, R. (1999). *Hershey's Milk Chocolate Fractions Book*. Scholastic, Inc. ISBN 0439135192.

Pistoia, S. (2002). *Fractions*. Child's World, Inc. ISBN 1567661130.

Pizza Fractions

Color the pizza. Slice the pizza into assigned fractions.

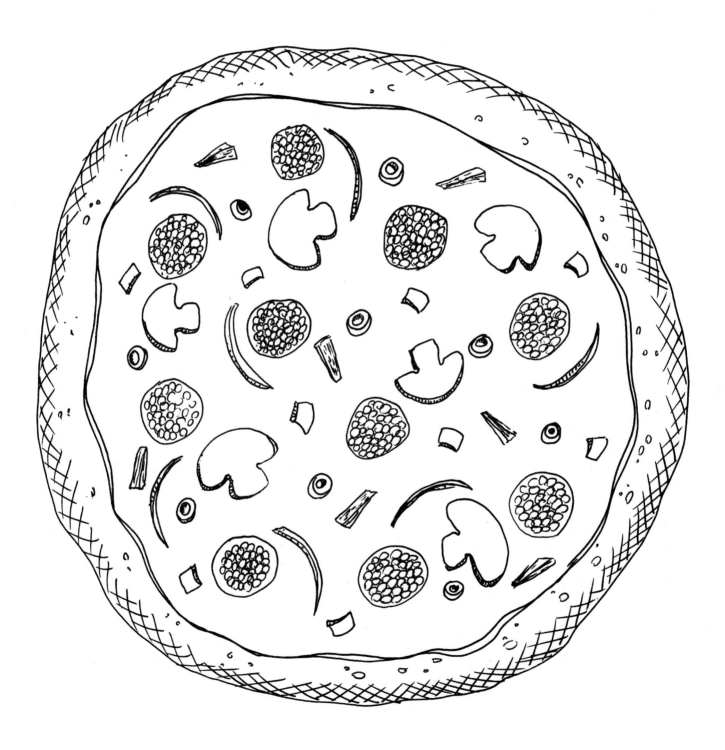

Pie Fractions

Color the pie. Cut the pie into assigned fractions.

Candy Bar Fractions

Color the candy bar. Divide the candy bar into assigned fractions.

Candy Bar Fractions

Cut the candy bars into assigned fractions and glue on the grid. Write the fraction below.

Candy Bar Fractions—
Grid Exercise (1 of 2)

MILK CHOCOLATE

MILK CHOCOLATE

MILK CHOCOLATE

MILK CHOCOLATE

MILK CHOCOLATE

MILK CHOCOLATE

MILK CHOCOLATE

MILK CHOCOLATE

Candy Bar Fractions—
Grid Exercise (2 of 2)

Fractions—Circle Models

Color to show fractions as dictated by the teacher.

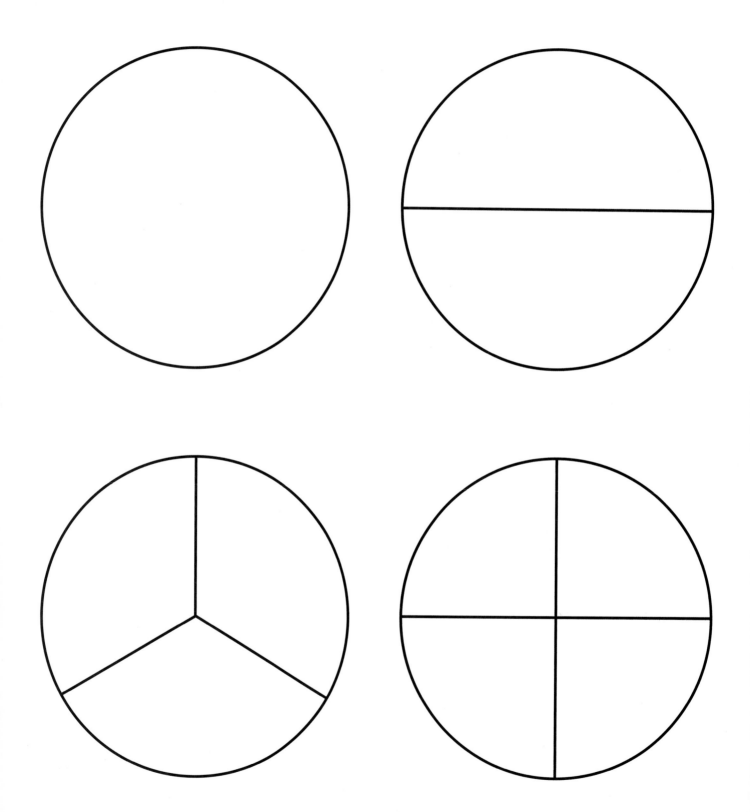

Fractions—Circle Models

Color to show fractions as dictated by the teacher.

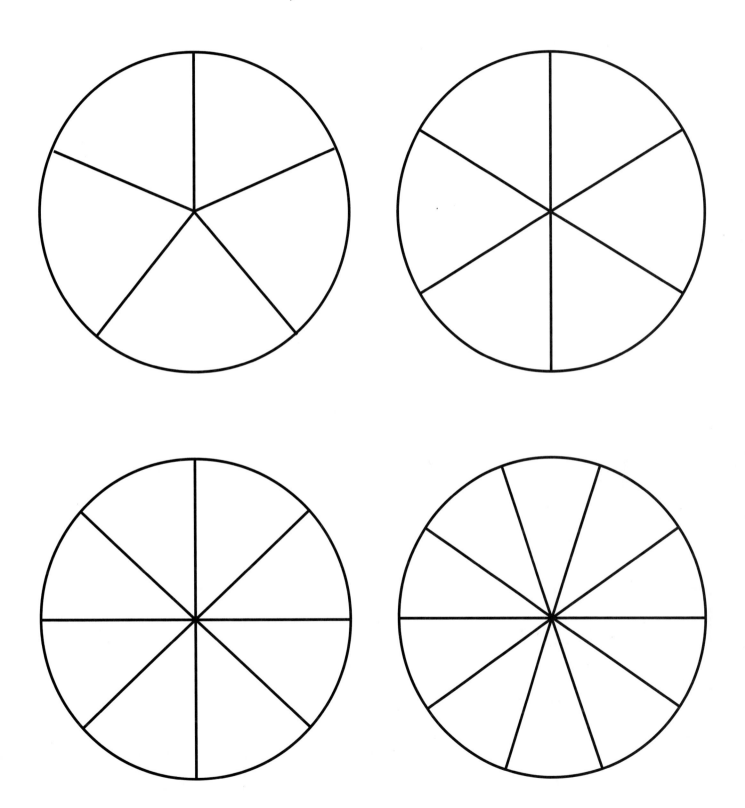

Fractions—Rectangle Models

Color to show fractions as dictated by the teacher.

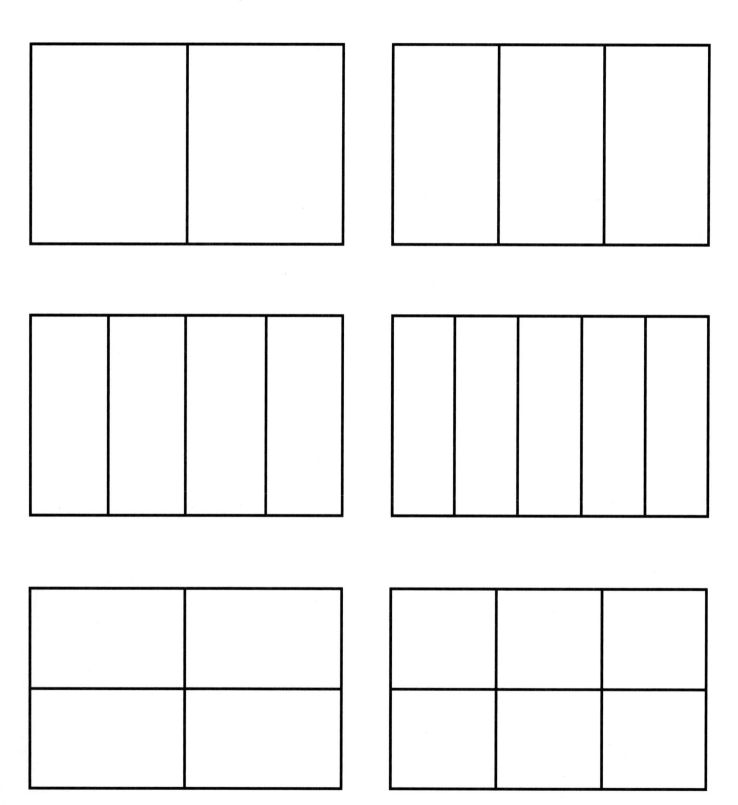

Fractions—Rectangle Models

Color to show fractions as dictated by the teacher.

Clocks

Learning to read the ordinary dial clock or watch is a complicated concept for young learners but one that is often taught early on. It is important to include several components when teaching the clock, such as the hour hand, minute hand, and second hand, as well as how the hands move in a circular fashion. The best way to teach these concepts is to use a large scale model of a clock. More important, it's critical that each child has his or her own clock to manipulate as the teacher demonstrates a specific time or adjustment.

Clocks are easy to make and become more meaningful when students create their own. Using a paper plate, some cutout hands, and a brad fastener, students can create their own clocks to practice telling time with. The following hands and numbers can be used in making your clock. The hands should be copied onto heavier paper to withstand heavy usage.

These books about clocks might be of use to you and your students:

Adam, W. (2000). *Telling Time.* Dover Publications. ISBN 0486407942.

Butterfield, M. (2000). *Learning Clock.* Barnes and Noble Books. ISBN 0760719160.

Older, J. (2000). *Telling Time.* Charlesbridge Publishing, Inc. ISBN 0881063975.

Talking Clock (2005). *Learning Resources.* ISBN 140063184X.

Wright, M. (2002). *Telling Time Games: Using the Judy Clock.* Frank Schaffer Publications. ISBN 0768227216.

Name: _____

Date: _____

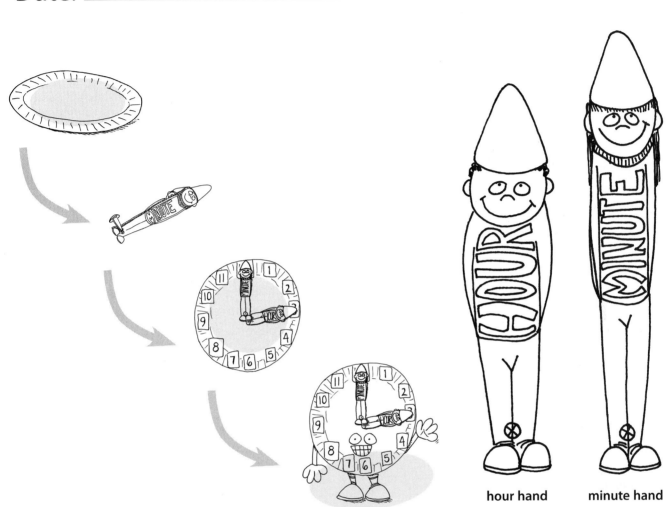

hour hand   minute hand

1	2	3	4	5	6
7	8	9	10	11	12

Pentominoes

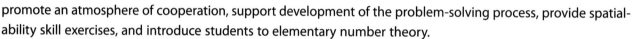

Pentominoes are shapes that use five square blocks joined together with at least one common side. There are 12 shapes in the set of pentominoes, named T, U, V, W, X, Y, Z, F, I, L, P, and N. Since there are 12 distinct pentomino shapes and each covers 5 squares, their total area is 60 squares. There are many 60-square grids available to use for challenging students' skills in connecting the shapes.

Pentominoes serve as fascinating "enrichment" material in school mathematics. There are at least five good reasons to incorporate pentominoes in the classroom. Pentominoes nurture a nonanxious attitude toward mathematics and science, promote an atmosphere of cooperation, support development of the problem-solving process, provide spatial-ability skill exercises, and introduce students to elementary number theory.

Pentomino activities provide good practice using the four-step problem-solving process, which includes understanding the problem, devising a plan, carrying out a plan, and checking the work. Besides its intrigue as a puzzle, the placement of pentominoes on a grid also makes it an exciting and competitive game of skill. Played by one, two, or three players, the object of the game is to be the last player to place a pentomino piece on the grid. Players take turns choosing a piece and placing it on the grid. The pieces must not overlap or extend beyond the boundary of the grid, but they do not have to be adjacent. When playing by oneself, the object is to complete the entire puzzle following the same criteria. (For more information, go to andrews.edu/~calkins/math/pentos .htm.)

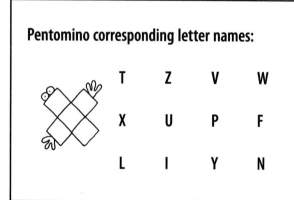

Pentomino corresponding letter names:

T	Z	V	W
X	U	P	F
L	I	Y	N

These books about pentominoes might be helpful to you and your students:

Hale, H. (1997). *Pentominoes*. Tarquin Publication, UK. ISBN 090621257X.
Problem Solving with Pentominoes (1993). Learning Resources, Inc. ISBN 1569119996.
Try It! Pentominoes (2000). Learning Resources, Inc. ISBN 1569110573.

Pentominoes

Color. Cut out the pentominoes. Arrange them to fill the pentomino grid (6 × 10 square grid).

Pentomino Grid

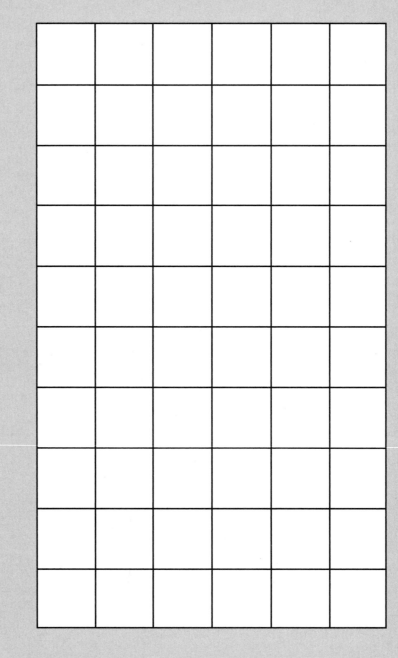

Money and Measurement

Money

Money is frequently used in teaching many areas of the mathematics curriculum. It's a great way to teach adding, subtracting, percents, fractions, and so on. The templates included in this book give students an opportunity to have coins available to them to learn just that.

Measurement

Measurement provides an excellent way to present problem-solving experiences at every level. Measurement is a fundamental component of the math curriculum for many reasons. It addresses applications for everyday life. It can be used to understand other types of math. It can easily link across the curriculum. And it keeps students engaged and participating. The following pages offer activities and tools in which to include students actively in their learning of measurement.

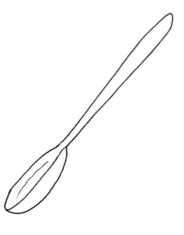

Money

Create your own money set. Color and cut out the money. Practice counting various amounts of money.

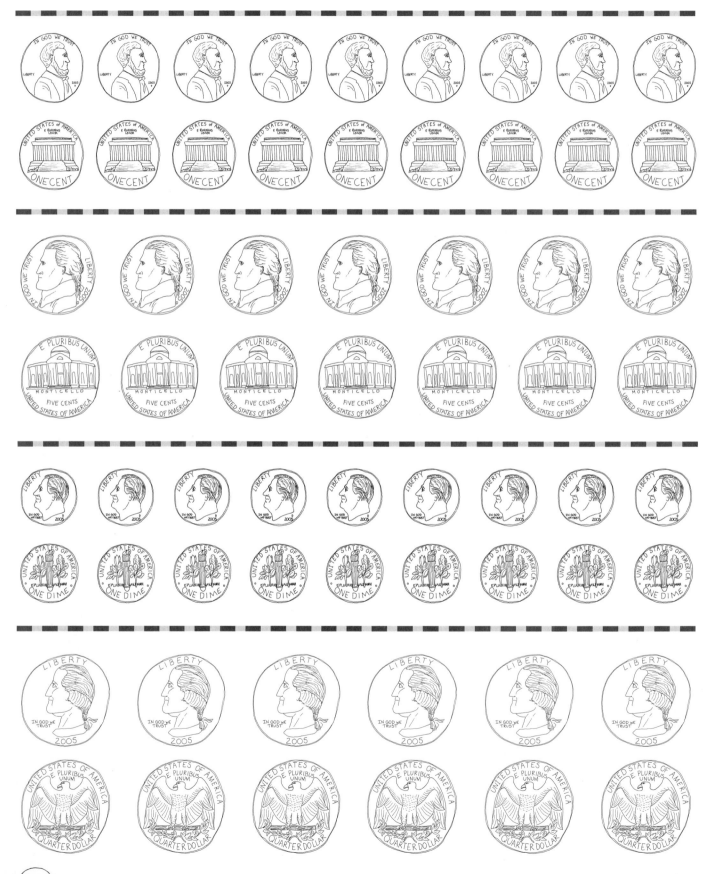

Volume

Color each unit of measure a designated color.

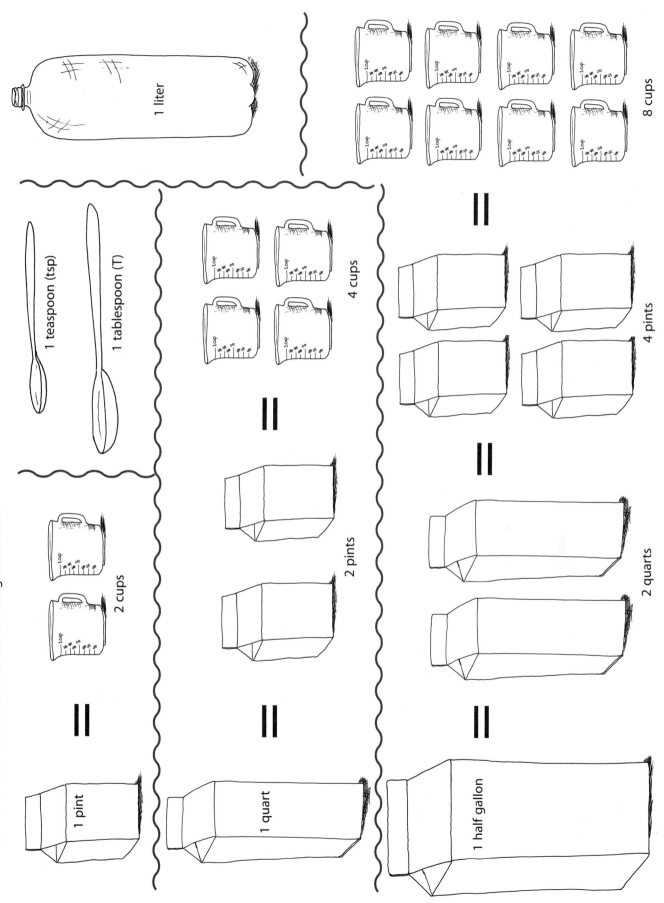

1 liter

8 cups

=

4 cups

4 pints

=

=

1 teaspoon (tsp)

1 tablespoon (T)

2 cups

2 pints

2 quarts

=

=

=

1 pint

1 quart

1 half gallon

© McGraw-Hill Education

Volume

Color each unit of measure a designated color.

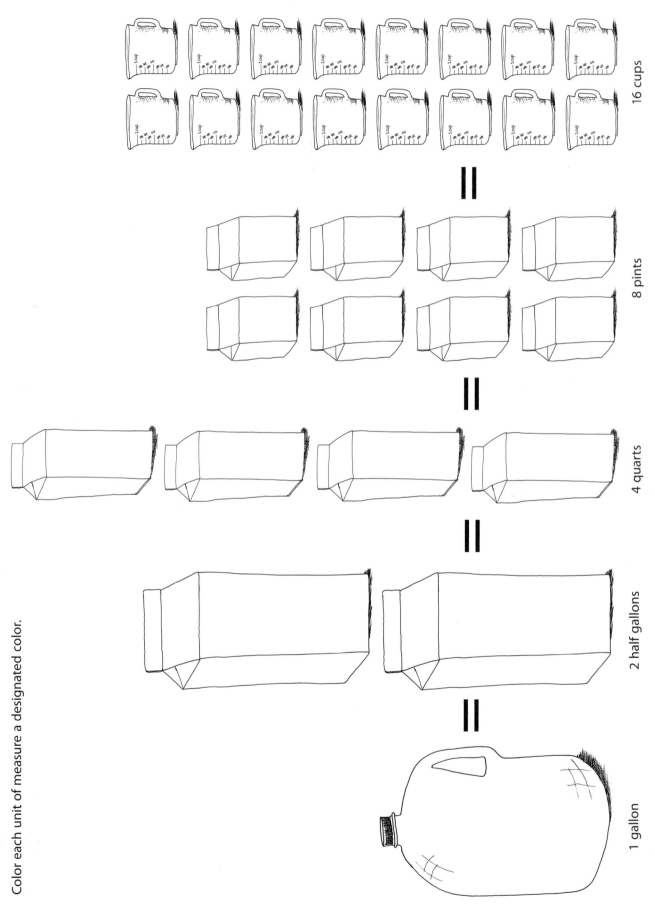

16 cups

$=$

8 pints

$=$

4 quarts

$=$

2 half gallons

$=$

1 gallon

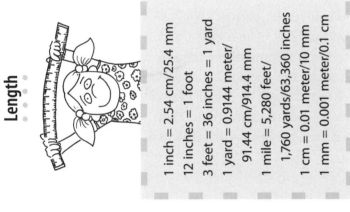

inches

Length

1 inch = 2.54 cm/25.4 mm
12 inches = 1 foot
3 feet = 36 inches = 1 yard
1 yard = 0.9144 meter/
91.44 cm/914.4 mm
1 mile = 5,280 feet/
1,760 yards/63,360 inches
1 cm = 0.01 meter/10 mm
1 mm = 0.001 meter/0.1 cm

Weight

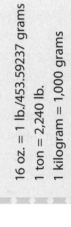

16 oz. = 1 lb./453.59237 grams
1 ton = 2,240 lb.
1 kilogram = 1,000 grams

Temperature

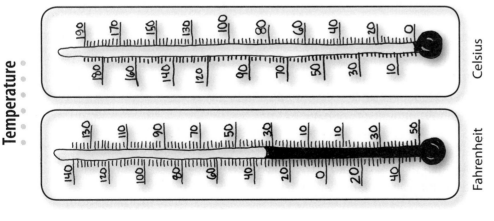

Celsius

Fahrenheit

	F	C
Boiling	212°	100°
Freezing	32°	0°

$$C = \frac{5}{9}\,(°F - 32)$$
$$F = \frac{9}{5}\,(°C) + 32$$

Graphing

Graphing skills include constructing and reading graphs as well as interpreting graphical information. There are several types of graphs, including picture graphs, pie or circle graphs, bar graphs, line graphs, or stem-and-leaf plots.

Picture Graphs Data are represented by pictures. A picture can represent one object or several. Children must know how much each object represents in order to interpret picture graphs.

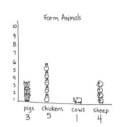

Pie/Circle Graphs Pie or circle graphs are useful when determining what portion of a whole are represented. Wedges report percentages of the whole. The pie graph is popular because it is easy to interpret, but it has limitations because it cannot exceed 100 percent. Usually a legend is near the pie chart to identify which color stands for which category. In addition, the percents are also near the pie slice that stands for that particular part of the whole being represented.

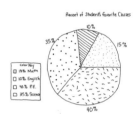

Bar Graphs Bar graphs are an excellent way to show one-time results, such as with surveys, inventories, and so on. A bar chart is marked off with a series of lines called grid lines. These lines typically indicate a numerical point in the series of numbers on the axis or line. More grid lines make it easier to be exact with the amounts being shown on the bar graph, but too many can make it confusing. Bar graphs are useful to get an overall idea of trends in responses, for example, which categories get more responses than others. They are also useful for quick visual comparisons of categories of data, but line graphs are more effective for showing trends over time.

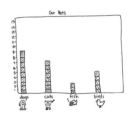

Line Graphs A line graph is useful in showing data that change over time. Points on a grid are used to represent continuous data. Each axis is labeled so the data shown can be interpreted properly. Line graphs are good for showing variations such as hours of daylight, temperature, or snowfall. They are also good for visually comparing many sets of data. Children must examine both vertical and horizontal axes.

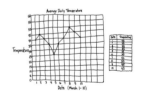

Stem-and-Leaf Plots In a stem-and-leaf plot, each data value is split into a "stem" and a "leaf." The "leaf" is usually the last digit of the number, and the other digits to the left of the "leaf" form the "stem." Stem-and-leaf plots show the shape and distribution of data. They are often used in magazines and newspapers since they provide efficient ways of showing information as well as comparing different sets of data.

Reading Quiz Scores/50	
Stem	Leaf
2	8, 9
3	5, 5, 8
4	4, 6, 6, 7, 8
5	0, 0, 0, 0

Legend: 4 | 6 means 46

- The *leaf* is the digit in the place farthest to the right in the number, and the *stem* is the digit, or digits, in the number that remains when the leaf is dropped. Stem: 3 Leaf: 8 = 38
- To show a one-digit number (such as 9) using a stem-and-leaf plot, use a stem of 0 and a leaf of 9.
- To find the median in a stem-and-leaf plot, count off half the total number of leaves.

My Picture Graph

Title graph.
Label graph.
Glue/attach grouped objects in columns.

Name: _____

Date: _____

Title: _____

10

9

8

7

6

5

4

3

2

1

Pie/Circle Graph

Name:

Date:

Title:

Title graph.
Divide into wedges that represent percentages of the whole.
Color wedges.
Label color key.

Color Key

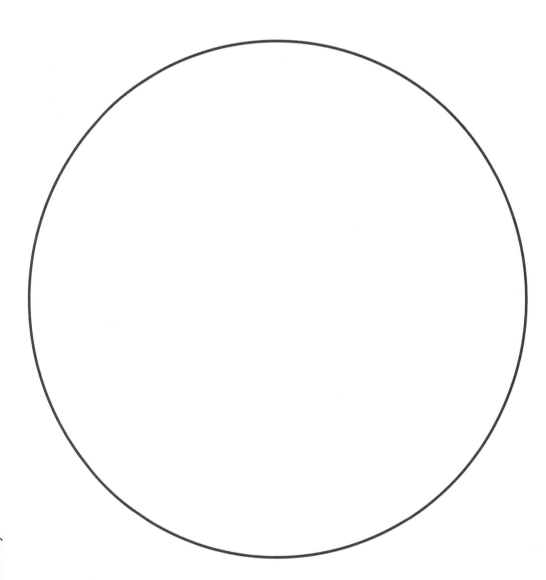

Bar Graph

Name:

Date:

Title:

Title graph.
Label each axis.
Color corresponding number of boxes for data.

Line Graph

Name:

Date:

Title:

Title your graph.

Label each axis.

Plot coordinate points on grid.

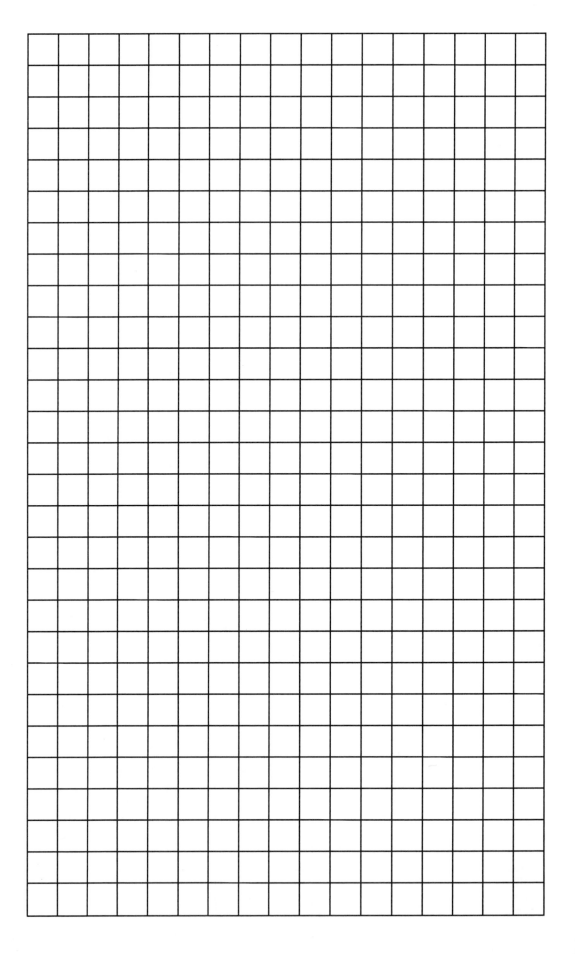

Stem-and-Leaf Plot

Name: _____

Date: _____

Title: _____

Title your graph.
Label each axis.
Plot coordinate points on grid.

Numeric Order of Data

Write data in numerical order (e.g., 35, 36, 39, 40, 41, 43, 49, 53, 57, 59).

_____

_____

_____

Legend (e.g., 3|6 means 36)

_____

Example

Title: *Quiz Scores*

Stem	Leaf
3	5, 6, 9
4	0, 1, 3, 9
5	3, 7, 9

Stem-and-Leaf Grouping

Title: _____

Stem	Leaf

Tens Frames

Tens frames are excellent learning tools for primary addition and subtraction. Students can conceptualize the concept of tens and ones. Using manipulatives to fill the tens frame, students learn that making ten and then counting the remainders is a valuable tool in solving addition problems between 10 and 20.

The following tens frame can be reproduced on heavier paper and even laminated for use from year to year.

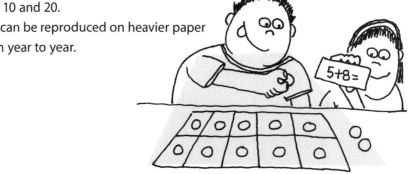

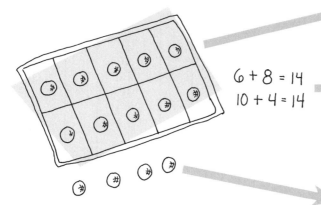

Mount on a colored piece of construction paper and laminate for durability.

$$6 + 8 = 14$$
$$10 + 4 = 14$$

Great for addition and subtraction of numbers between 10 and 20.

Use any kind of manipulative. It is always a good idea to familiarize students with manipulatives first.

Hundreds Charts

Hundreds charts are a powerful math learning tool. There are numerous activities that can be done with hundreds charts to strengthen a student's number concepts and counting patterns. There are several hundreds chart templates in this section, and suggested activities are listed below. These activities can be printed and used by students or even made into overheads for whole group activities. The charts can be colored or markers can be laid on them for designated counting patterns.

- Color every 2, 3, 4, 5, and so on, to practice counting patterns.

- Look for patterns. Rows have the same number in the tens. Columns have the same number in the ones position.

- Use to practice + and −, counting on and counting back.

- Mark patterns. Draw circles around even numbers and squares around odd numbers. Draw triangles around numbers that count in 5s, etc.

- Count 1 more, 1 less, 10 more, 10 less, and so on.

- Complete partial hundreds chart and blank hundreds chart.

Hundreds Chart

Name:
Date:

1	2	3	4	5	6	7	8	9	10
11	12	13	14	15	16	17	18	19	20
21	22	23	24	25	26	27	28	29	30
31	32	33	34	35	36	37	38	39	40
41	42	43	44	45	46	47	48	49	50
51	52	53	54	55	56	57	58	59	60
61	62	63	64	65	66	67	68	69	70
71	72	73	74	75	76	77	78	79	80
81	82	83	84	85	86	87	88	89	90
91	92	93	94	95	96	97	98	99	100

Hundreds Chart

Name: _____

Date: _____

1	2	3	4	5	6	7	8	9	10
11	12	13	14	15	16	17	18	19	20
21	22	23	24	25	26	27	28	29	30
31	32	33	34	35	36	37	38	39	40
41	42	43	44	45	46	47	48	49	50
51	52	53	54	55	56	57	58	59	60
61	62	63	64	65	66	67	68	69	70
71	72	73	74	75	76	77	78	79	80
81	82	83	84	85	86	87	88	89	90
91	92	93	94	95	96	97	98	99	100

Hundreds Chart

Name: _____

Date: _____

1	2		4	5		7	8		10
11		13	14		16	17		19	20
21	22	23		25	26	27		29	30
	32		34	35		37	38	39	
41		43		45		47	48	49	50
51	52		54	55	56		58		60
61		63	64		66	67	68	69	
71	72	73		75	76	77		79	80
	82		84	85	86			89	90
91	92	93		95		97	98		100

Hundreds Chart

Name: _____

Date: _____

Hundreds Chart

Name: _____

Date: _____

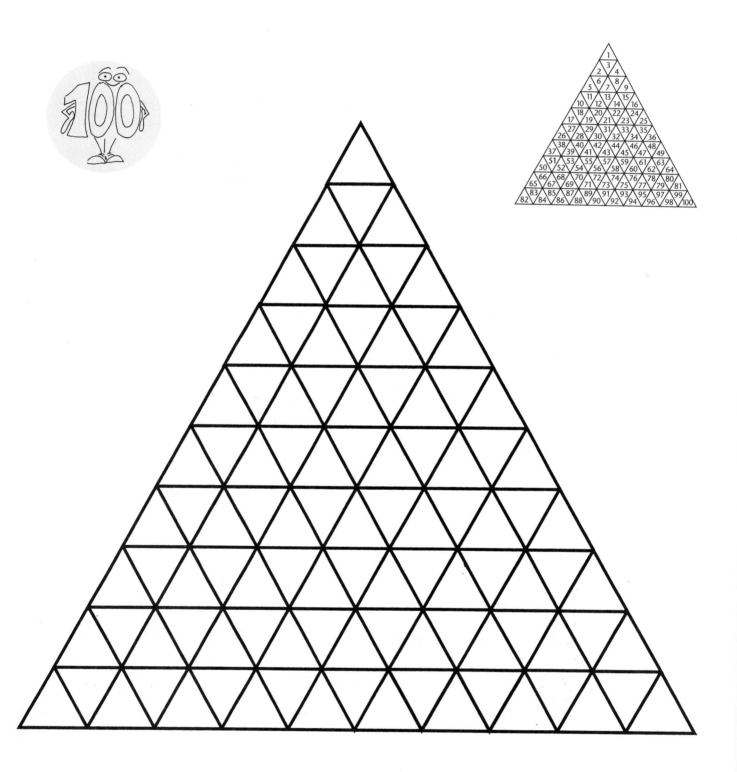

© McGraw-Hill Education

MULTIPLICATION TABLE

✕	1	2	3	4	5	6	7	8	9	10	11	12
1	1	2	3	4	5	6	7	8	9	10	11	12
2	2	4	6	8	10	12	14	16	18	20	22	24
3	3	6	9	12	15	18	21	24	27	30	33	36
4	4	8	12	16	20	24	28	32	36	40	44	48
5	5	10	15	20	25	30	35	40	45	50	55	60
6	6	12	18	24	30	36	42	48	54	60	66	72
7	7	14	21	28	35	42	49	56	63	70	77	84
8	8	16	24	32	40	48	56	64	72	80	88	96
9	9	18	27	36	45	54	63	72	81	90	99	108
10	10	20	30	40	50	60	70	80	90	100	110	120
11	11	22	33	44	55	66	77	88	99	110	121	132
12	12	24	36	48	60	72	84	96	108	120	132	144

Flash Cards

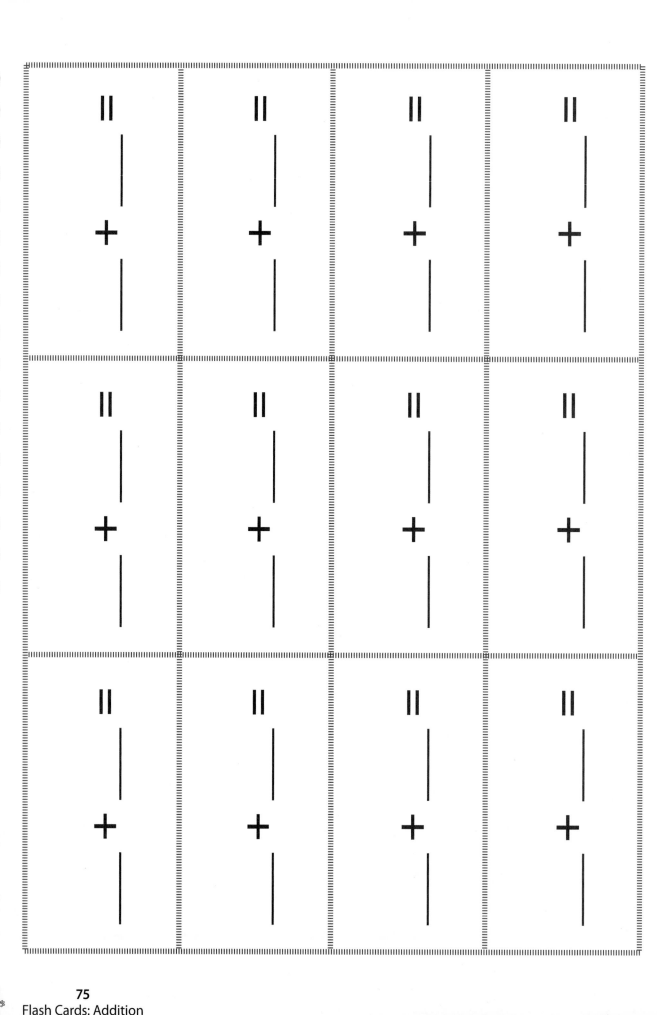

Flash Cards

Flash Cards

Create your own set of multiplication flash cards (e.g., 2 × 2 = 4, 2 × 3 = 6, 2 × 4 = 8).

___ × ___ =	___ × ___ =	___ × ___ =	___ × ___ =
___ × ___ =	___ × ___ =	___ × ___ =	___ × ___ =
___ × ___ =	___ × ___ =	___ × ___ =	___ × ___ =

Flash Cards

Create your own set of division flash cards (e.g., 24 ÷ 2 = 12, 22 ÷ 2 = 11, 20 ÷ 2 = 10).

	÷	=
	÷	=
	÷	=
	÷	=
	÷	=
	÷	=
	÷	=
	÷	=
	÷	=
	÷	=
	÷	=
	÷	=

Calendars

Calendars are powerful learning tools, and involving students in the calendar makes for meaningful, purposeful learning. Most classrooms have a calendar on the wall or attached to the whiteboard or portable stand. Many students even enjoy helping create the classroom calendar. Maintaining the personal calendars can also be a powerful learning experience for students. The following pages are calendar templates that can be used.

Student-Created Classroom Calendar Numbers

- Theme-related
- Season-related
- Holiday-related
- Art-related

Student Calendar

- Track weather
- Record homework
- Math tool: patterns, number of days in school
- Theme-based: curriculum-related topic
- Activity-based
- Word of the Day
- Track school/classroom news: field trips, days off, assemblies, and so forth

112

YEAR _____

JANUARY	FEBRUARY	MARCH	APRIL
MAY	JUNE	JULY	AUGUST
SEPTEMBER	OCTOBER	NOVEMBER	DECEMBER

Sunday	Monday	Tuesday	Wednesday	Thursday	Friday	Saturday

Story Problems

The following pages consist of blank templates for students to create math story problems. You can assign specific scenes or let the children choose. Have them switch stories with a partner after they are done and let the partner complete the story problem.

My Story Problem

Name: _____

Date: _____

Use barnyard template to create a math story problem and illustrate.

_____ (_____) _____ = _____

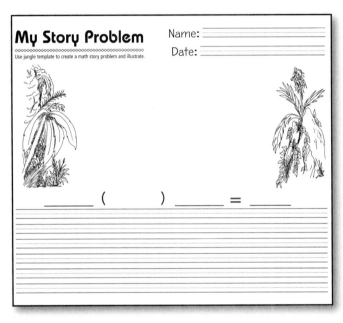

My Story Problem

Name: _____

Date: _____

Use jungle template to create a math story problem and illustrate.

_____ (_____) _____ = _____

My Story Problem

Name: _____

Date: _____

Use space template to create a math story problem and illustrate.

_____ (_____) _____ = _____

My Story Problem

Name: _____

Date: _____

Use ocean template to create a math story problem and illustrate.

_____ (_____) _____ = _____

My Story Problem

Use this barnyard template to create a math story problem and illustrate.

Name: _____

Date: _____

( ) =

My Story Problem: Barnyard Template

My Story Problem

Use this jungle template to create a math story problem and illustrate.

Name: _____

Date: _____

(_____ (_____) = _____

My Story Problem: Jungle Template

My Story Problem

Name:

Date:

Use this space template to create a math story problem and illustrate.

$$\underline{\hphantom{XXXX}} \; (\; \underline{\hphantom{XXXX}} \;) \; = \; \underline{\hphantom{XXXX}}$$

83
My Story Problem: Space Template

© McGraw-Hill Education

My Story Problem

Use this ocean template to create a math story problem and illustrate.

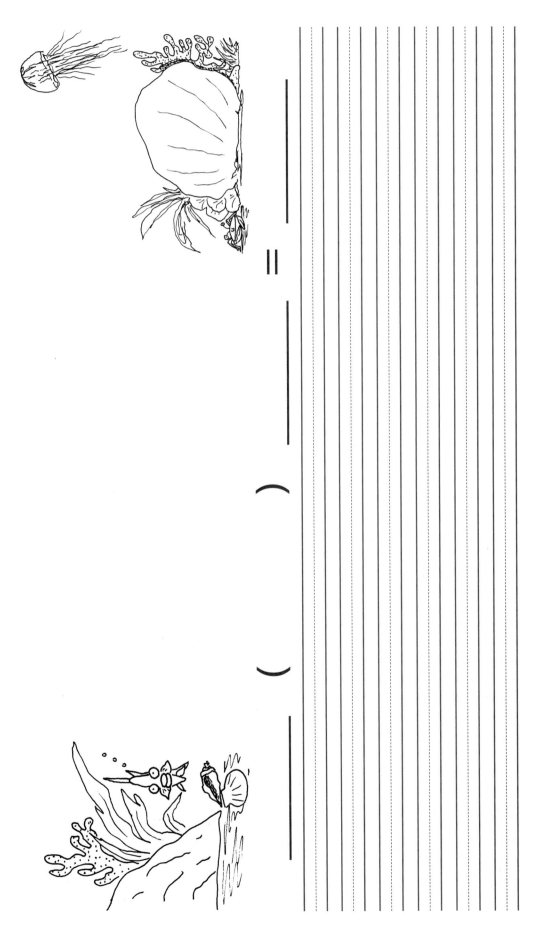

(   )   (   ) = _____

My Story Problem

Create a math story problem and illustrate your own scene.

$$(\quad\rule{3cm}{0.4pt}\quad) = \rule{3cm}{0.4pt}$$

Name: _____

Date: _____

Number of the Day

Name: _____

Date: _____

_____

Spell it. _____

| 1 more = _____ | 1 less = _____ | | TALLIES |

10 more = _____   10 less = _____

TENS	ONES	FACT FAMILY	
		_____ + _____ = _____	_____ > _____
		_____ + _____ = _____	
		_____ − _____ = _____	_____ < _____
		_____ − _____ = _____	_____ = _____

On the back, write and illustrate a story problem using the number of the day.

- -

Number of the Day

Name: _____

Date: _____

_____

Spell it. _____

1 more = _____   1 less = _____   TALLIES

10 more = _____   10 less = _____

TENS	ONES	FACT FAMILY	
		_____ + _____ = _____	_____ > _____
		_____ + _____ = _____	
		_____ − _____ = _____	_____ < _____
		_____ − _____ = _____	_____ = _____

On the back, write and illustrate a story problem using the number of the day.

Number of the Day

_____
- - - - - -
_____

Name: _____

Date: _____

_____

Spell it. _____

| 1 more = ____ | 2 more = ____ | 10 more = ____ |
| 1 less = ____ | 2 less = ____ | 10 less = ____ |

TALLIES

HUNDREDS	TENS	ONES

FACT FAMILY

____ + ____ = ____
____ + ____ = ____
____ − ____ = ____
____ − ____ = ____

____ > ____

____ < ____

____ = ____

ROUNDING

Round to the nearest . . .

ten _____

hundred _____

On the back, write and illustrate a story problem using the number of the day.

- -

Number of the Day

_____
- - - - - -
_____

Name: _____

Date: _____

_____

Spell it. _____

| 1 more = ____ | 2 more = ____ | 10 more = ____ |
| 1 less = ____ | 2 less = ____ | 10 less = ____ |

TALLIES

HUNDREDS	TENS	ONES

FACT FAMILY

____ + ____ = ____
____ + ____ = ____
____ − ____ = ____
____ − ____ = ____

____ > ____

____ < ____

____ = ____

ROUNDING

Round to the nearest . . .

ten _____

hundred _____

On the back, write and illustrate a story problem using the number of the day.

Number of the Day

Name: _____

Date: _____

_____

Spell it. _____

10 more = _____   100 more = _____   1,000 more = _____

10 less = _____   100 less = _____   1,000 less = _____

THOUSANDS	HUNDREDS	TENS	ONES

FACT FAMILY

_____ × _____ = _____

_____ × _____ = _____

_____ ÷ _____ = _____

_____ ÷ _____ = _____

_____ > _____

_____ < _____

_____ = _____

EXPANDED NOTATION

ROUNDING

Round to the nearest . . .

ten   _____

hundred   _____

thousand   _____

On the back, write and illustrate a story problem using the number of the day.

- -

Number of the Day

Name: _____

Date: _____

_____

Spell it. _____

10 more = _____   100 more = _____   1,000 more = _____

10 less = _____   100 less = _____   1,000 less = _____

THOUSANDS	HUNDREDS	TENS	ONES

FACT FAMILY

_____ × _____ = _____

_____ × _____ = _____

_____ ÷ _____ = _____

_____ ÷ _____ = _____

_____ > _____

_____ < _____

_____ = _____

EXPANDED NOTATION

ROUNDING

Round to the nearest . . .

ten   _____

hundred   _____

thousand   _____

On the back, write and illustrate a story problem using the number of the day.

Writing

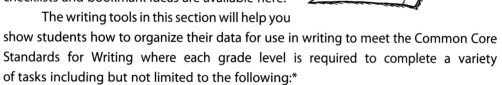

In this section, you will find a variety of "out of the box" writing experiences—from "Word of the Day" to story-starter prompts, Graphic Organizers, and engaging writing ideas. Help your students assess their writer identity with the survey and inventories. You'll also want to share the "Autobiography" recipe, classroom newspaper, and "Create a Menu" with your class. Additionally, proofreading/editing/writing checklists and bookmark ideas are available here.

The writing tools in this section will help you show students how to organize their data for use in writing to meet the Common Core Standards for Writing where each grade level is required to complete a variety of tasks including but not limited to the following:*

1. **Text types and purposes.** Students deliver opinion pieces on topics or texts; support a point of view; write from perspectives such as informative, explanatory, narratives, or persuasive; and more. These concepts increase with intensity and detailed mechanics as students move through the grades.

2. **Production and distribution of writing.** Beginning in the early grades, students respond to questions and suggestions, add details to strengthen writing, move through the writing process from development to publishing, and use technology in the upper grades to produce finished products.

3. **Research to build and present knowledge.** Using fiction and nonfiction books in the early grades to express opinions, sequence instructions and events, and respond to questions are typical research skills. This continues into the middle grades and also includes using a number of books on a single topic to produce a report, record science observations, and recall information. Moving to the upper grades, where students continue using said materials to write, they also take notes on sources and sort evidence into categories, conduct research projects, and draw evidence from literary and informational texts to support analysis, reflection, and research.

4. **Range of writing.** Beginning in third grade, students write over extended periods (time for research, reflection, and revision) and shorter periods (a single sitting or a day or two) for a range of tasks, purposes, and audiences.

---

*For more about grade level writing standards, visit the CCS website at http://www.core standards.org/the-standards.

Name: _____ Date: _____

Writing Interest Inventory

Circle your answer.

1. I enjoy writing.   YES   NO   MAYBE

2. I like to share what I write with others.   YES   NO   MAYBE

3. I feel like a real author when I write.   YES   NO   MAYBE

4. My family likes to read my writing.   YES   NO   MAYBE

5. I like when others help me with my writing.   YES   NO   MAYBE

6. The hardest thing about writing for me is _____

_____

_____

Here is a sample of my writing.

Name: _____ Date: _____

Writing Survey

Please answer all of the questions below in complete sentences.

1. Have you ever considered yourself an author? If so, when? What was your writing about?

   _____

   _____

2. Why do you think people like to write? _____

   _____

3. Do you think most people like to write? Why or why not? _____

   _____

4. Do your parents write? If so, what do they write about? _____

   _____

5. Who is your favorite author? Why? _____

   _____

6. Are there any books by a certain author that have helped you with your writing?

   Who is the author, and how did he or she help? _____

   _____

7. How do you come up with your ideas about what to write? _____

   _____

8. What are your favorite topics to write about? _____

   _____

9. Where is your favorite place to write? _____

   _____

10. When is the best time of day for you to write? _____

    _____

11. Is there anything you do to help you get excited about writing? _____

    _____

Name: _____ Date: _____

How I See Myself as a Writer

Please answer all of the questions below in complete sentences.

 1. What are your strengths as a writer?

_____

_____

 2. What type of writing do you like to do best?

_____

_____

 3. What are some important things to keep in mind as you write?

_____

_____

 4. Explain a time when you experienced a positive writing experience in which you really enjoyed what you were writing.

_____

_____

 5. What are some things you need to do in order to improve your writing?

_____

_____

 6. Explain the things you know about the writing process.

_____

_____

 7. Explain what you know about graphic organizers.

_____

_____

 8. What do you like to write most about?

_____

_____

Name: _____ Date: _____

Self-Editing and Peer-Editing Checklist

Check the box as you finish each step.

☐ 1. When you finish your rough draft, make the necessary corrections using the checklist.

☐ 2. After you have edited your paper, trade it with a friend and make corrections on each other's papers.

☐ 3. After you have edited your friend's paper, trade back and write your second draft. When you have finished writing your second draft, make any final edits.

☐ 4. When you have completed your second editing, go ahead and publish your final essay.

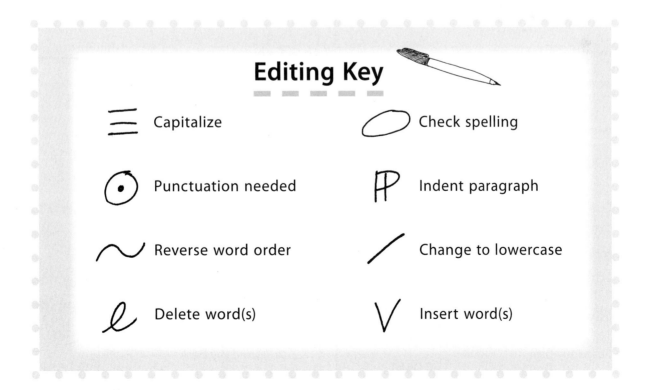

Editing Key

≡ Capitalize ⬭ Check spelling

⊙ Punctuation needed ⫪ Indent paragraph

∼ Reverse word order / Change to lowercase

ℓ Delete word(s) ⋁ Insert word(s)

Primary Writer's Checklist

Writer's Checklist

Assignment: _____

Check your work!

_____ I started my sentences with capital letters.

_____ I used punctuation marks.

_____ I used details.

_____ My sentences relate to my topic.

_____ I checked my spelling.

_____ I shared my writing.

_____ I used my best handwriting.

Writer's Checklist

Assignment: _____

Check your work!

_____ I started my sentences with capital letters.

_____ I used punctuation marks.

_____ I used details.

_____ My sentences relate to my topic.

_____ I checked my spelling.

_____ I shared my writing.

_____ I used my best handwriting.

Writer's Checklist

Assignment: _____

Check your work!

_____ I started my sentences with capital letters.

_____ I used punctuation marks.

_____ I used details.

_____ My sentences relate to my topic.

_____ I checked my spelling.

_____ I shared my writing.

_____ I used my best handwriting.

Writer's Checklist

Assignment: _____

Check your work!

_____ I started my sentences with capital letters.

_____ I used punctuation marks.

_____ I used details.

_____ My sentences relate to my topic.

_____ I checked my spelling.

_____ I shared my writing.

_____ I used my best handwriting.

Advanced Writer's Checklist

Writer's Checklist

Assignment: _____

First, check the elements of focus for this assignment. Later, check off those items as they are completed.

FOCUS ELEMENTS **CHECK OFF ITEMS**

_____ Good sentence structure ☐

_____ Proper punctuation ☐

_____ Good leads/openings ☐

_____ Voice ☐

_____ Good transitions/flow ☐

_____ Details ☐

_____ On topic/focused ☐

_____ Handwriting ☐

_____ Organization ☐

_____ Descriptive/word choice ☐

_____ Spelling ☐

Writer's Checklist

Assignment: _____

First, check the elements of focus for this assignment. Later, check off those items as they are completed.

FOCUS ELEMENTS **CHECK OFF ITEMS**

_____ Good sentence structure ☐

_____ Proper punctuation ☐

_____ Good leads/openings ☐

_____ Voice ☐

_____ Good transitions/flow ☐

_____ Details ☐

_____ On topic/focused ☐

_____ Handwriting ☐

_____ Organization ☐

_____ Descriptive/word choice ☐

_____ Spelling ☐

Writer's Checklist

Assignment: _____

First, check the elements of focus for this assignment. Later, check off those items as they are completed.

FOCUS ELEMENTS **CHECK OFF ITEMS**

_____ Good sentence structure ☐

_____ Proper punctuation ☐

_____ Good leads/openings ☐

_____ Voice ☐

_____ Good transitions/flow ☐

_____ Details ☐

_____ On topic/focused ☐

_____ Handwriting ☐

_____ Organization ☐

_____ Descriptive/word choice ☐

_____ Spelling ☐

Writer's Checklist

Assignment: _____

First, check the elements of focus for this assignment. Later, check off those items as they are completed.

FOCUS ELEMENTS **CHECK OFF ITEMS**

_____ Good sentence structure ☐

_____ Proper punctuation ☐

_____ Good leads/openings ☐

_____ Voice ☐

_____ Good transitions/flow ☐

_____ Details ☐

_____ On topic/focused ☐

_____ Handwriting ☐

_____ Organization ☐

_____ Descriptive/word choice ☐

_____ Spelling ☐

Word of the Day

Name: _____

Date: _____

_____

Complete all possible information for Word of the Day.

ILLUSTRATION

Part of Speech: ☐ Noun ☐ Verb ☐ Adjective

Number of: Consonants _____ Vowels _____

Syllables _____ Sounds (phonemes) _____

DEFINITION _____

Prefix: _____ Suffix: _____

Rhyming Word(s): _____

Antonym: _____ Synonym: _____

MEANINGFUL SENTENCE

LIFTED EXAMPLE: STORY/PASSAGE _____ **PAGE:** _____

Bookmark

Comprehension is the key to good reading. Students need to be able to understand what they have read. The following bookmarks can be photocopied on heavy card stock and used to check comprehension. They make great tools for parents as they check their child's understanding of a book. In addition, they can be used as a guide for writing book reports and book summaries.

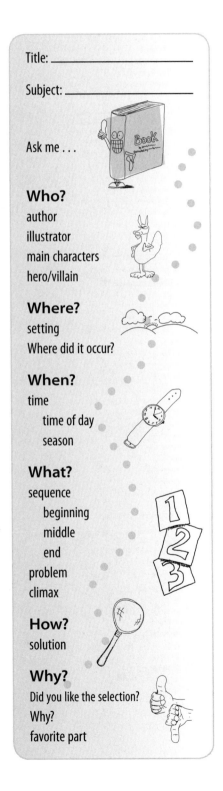

Title: _____

Subject: _____

Ask me . . .

Who?
author
illustrator
main characters
hero/villain

Where?
setting
Where did it occur?

When?
time
    time of day
    season

What?
sequence
    beginning
    middle
    end
problem
climax

How?
solution

Why?
Did you like the selection?
Why?
favorite part

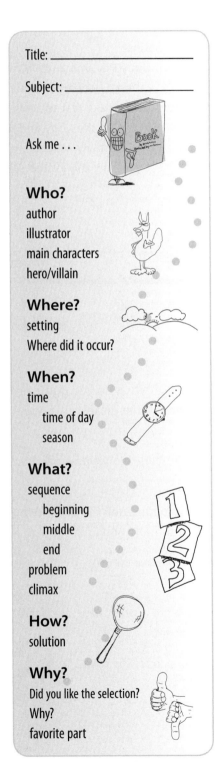

Title: _____

Subject: _____

Ask me . . .

Who?
author
illustrator
main characters
hero/villain

Where?
setting
Where did it occur?

When?
time
    time of day
    season

What?
sequence
    beginning
    middle
    end
problem
climax

How?
solution

Why?
Did you like the selection?
Why?
favorite part

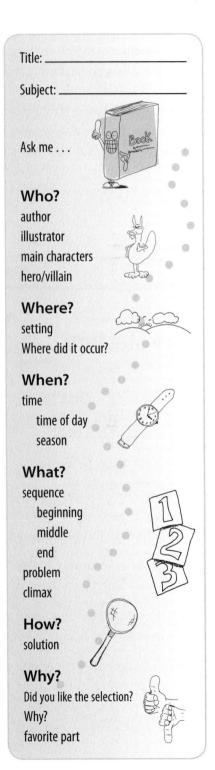

Title: _____

Subject: _____

Ask me . . .

Who?
author
illustrator
main characters
hero/villain

Where?
setting
Where did it occur?

When?
time
    time of day
    season

What?
sequence
    beginning
    middle
    end
problem
climax

How?
solution

Why?
Did you like the selection?
Why?
favorite part

Story Starters for Daily Journal Writing

Story starters are simple, fun, and creative ways to get your students geared up to begin their reading or writing for the day. You can use them in the morning when your students arrive and you have to take attendance, collect homework, and talk with parents. Story starters are meant to involve the creative writing aspect and can easily be contained in a journal. After 10 or 15 minutes, you may want to choose three to five students to share their stories, before moving on to the daily curriculum routine.

The following relatively simply story starters include silly, imaginative, nonsensical, and reflective ways to get your students excited about writing. Encourage students to have fun with these stories even if that means their writing doesn't make real sense in the real world. Remember, this is creative writing. It's only meant to warm up the body and mind to get the day started. It's also a nice way to transition back into the daily schedule after lunch and recess. The list below includes enough story starters for each day of the school year, with some extra in case you want more variety.

Story Starters

1. Imagine you are a dolphin. What do you look like? What do you do all day? What interesting things do you see? What worries you? What makes you happy? Use your answers to write a story.

2. Use these words to write about a witch: *cackle, scary, broom, brew, fly, black hat,* and *pointed nose and chin.*

3. The rain started to fall right after the lightning brightened the sky and the thunder blasted. When the electricity went out, my best friend and I . . .

4. I woke up this morning and realized I was five inches tall. Why did this happen? What will I do?

5. Use the following words about the beach to write a story: *sand, shells, ocean, waves, fun, seaweed, family, pail, shovel,* and *boogie board.*

6. Once I dreamed my cat could talk. She was hilarious. She said . . .

7. My brother/sister and I were walking along the sidewalk when all of a sudden it turned into grape soda. We . . .

8. Imagine you are a black widow spider. What do you look like? What do you do all day? What interesting things do you see? What do you worry about? What makes you happy? What makes you sad? Use your answers to write a story.

9. Use the following words about the park to write a short story: *slides, trees, swings, sand, squirrels, kids,* and *jungle gym.*

10. I finally came in first place and received the golden trophy. I was able to call any person in the world to share the news, and I dialed the number to . . .

11. My family took a safari tour of Africa. I heard something behind me coming from the dense jungle. As I opened my mouth to yell, out of the jungle came . . .

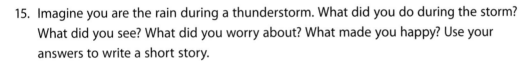

12. Imagine you are on a backpacking trip. Use the following words to write a story: *tent, woods, bears, squirrels, deer, caves, trees, ants,* and *food.*

13. I dreamed I was locked in a Target store for the night. I had a blast . . .

14. My friend's dad is a scientist. He took us for a ride in his time machine, and we went back in time to . . .

15. Imagine you are the rain during a thunderstorm. What did you do during the storm? What did you see? What did you worry about? What made you happy? Use your answers to write a short story.

16. Use the following words about a chocolate cake to write a short story: *frosting, cake, dog, eggs, milk, sugar, spoon, trouble,* and *bake.*

17. At the ice cream counter I ordered _____. Then I walked out of the store on that hot day and . . .

18. To my friend _____, I want you to be happy today. Here are five things I really admire about you and why:

    (1) _____

    (2) _____

    (3) _____

    (4) _____

    (5) _____

19. If you could "cook up" a perfect day, what would the ingredients and the steps for mixing and cooking the recipe include? Use the words *cups, teaspoons, tablespoons, pinch, bowl, stir, pour,* and *bake.*

20. I have a dream to make this world a better place. I see us all . . .

21. I woke up this morning and heard on the news that school was cancelled. I . . .

22. I was home alone watching a funny movie on TV when the electricity suddenly went out. There was a scream, and then the telephone rang. I . . .

23. My brother was at the starting line. I knew he was excited. The gun went off and the bicycles began to roll forward all at the same time. Just when a ball crossed their paths . . .

24. While at the circus, the tightrope walker's foot slipped and . . .

25. The school was holding auditions for the school play. I tried out for the lead role knowing I was the best but . . .

26. On my last birthday, my parents gave me an enormous box tied with a giant red ribbon. I opened the gift only to find . . .

27. The new classroom snake escaped from its cage during math time. It . . .

28. We went on a field trip to the aquarium. When we returned to school, we realized Jennifer had never gotten on the bus. She . . .

29. Write a story titled "Dog Stops Burglar."

30. In complete sentences, use as many adjectives as you can to describe your favorite fruit. Don't name the fruit, but use enough adjectives to describe it in detail so the reader can guess it.

31. In complete sentences, describe the personality and characteristics of your favorite cartoon character without telling your readers who it is. Let them try to guess from your description.

32. Use direction words to write instructions so your friend can go from school to your house. Don't forget to include what type of transportation your friend should use. Some direction words you might use are: *above, behind, beside, left, right, near, next to, straight, veer.*

33. Using time-sequence words such as *after, before, finally, last, next, first, then,* and *at the same time* as well as times such as *20 minutes,* write directions for making a cake.

34. Write a narrative story about the best day of your life. Be specific and include details.

35. Sharks are strange-looking creatures . . .

36. Whales are enormous creatures. They . . .

37. My best friend and I were playing in an empty lot. We came across two large barrels with the word *Danger* on them. We . . .

38. I woke up suddenly to the bright colors of flames shooting from a roof two blocks away. I . . .

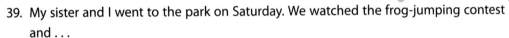

39. My sister and I went to the park on Saturday. We watched the frog-jumping contest and . . .

40. My black Labrador had puppies. We had to post a sign that announced free puppies. It said . . .

41. The year I was the school reporter is the same year we had a rat epidemic. I wrote the story, saying . . .

42. I bought a robot that was supposed to keep my room clean. When it arrived, I . . .

43. My little brothers and sisters are terrified of ghosts, so when we had to go to the haunted house up the street when the rain knocked out the phone lines, they . . .

44. My friend Jason always comes late. This time . . .

45. I would love to go on a field trip to Disneyland. If my class got to go . . .

46. It was Saturday morning but . . .

47. Basketball (or choose any sport) is my favorite sport because . . .

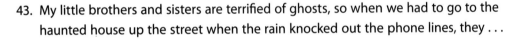

48. The first time I went ice skating, I didn't see the sign that read *Thin Ice.* My brothers and I skated for hours until . . .

49. Last night my friends and I dug up a time capsule by mistake. We opened it and found . . .

50. I received money to develop a new gadget. I bought springs, coil, rubber stoppers, and . . .

51. At the city fair, I watched the ice-cream sundae eating contest. The participants . . .

52. My dad bought my mom the largest diamond for her birthday. When she was in the shower one day, I tried it on. I guess I shouldn't have done so over the sink because . . .

53. If I were in charge of creating a new pizza, it would . . .

54. The school day should end right after lunch because . . .

55. My mom always makes us wear our seat belts, but one time . . .

56. Dear Mr. President, I don't understand . . . (be specific).

57. Dear Christopher Columbus, What I read about you in my Social Studies book is . . . (be specific).

58. Dear Martin Luther King Jr.: . . . (be specific).

59. Dear Principal: . . . (be specific).

60. Dear Mr./Mrs. (insert teacher's name), . . . (be specific).

61. I think we should eliminate the holiday _____, because . . .

62. I want to travel to the country of _____, because . . .

63. My best friend, Zeely, won't give up candy. Her parents and the dentist have told her _____, and I agree. Zeely is going to . . .

64. Last night my sister/brother and I argued about . . .

65. If I could eat _____ every day, I would . . .

66. The school year should be one month shorter because . . .

67. Cats make better pets than dogs . . .

68. Watching too much television and playing video games for too long, makes students' grades go down. I think . . .

69. Small children should not be left at home alone because . . .

70. My mom makes the best chocolate chip cookies. She . . .

71. If I had a choice between pizza and hamburgers, I would choose _____, because . . .

72. If I could have a baby koala bear as a pet, I would . . .

73. Have you ever seen an anaconda? It . . .

74. I opened my lunch box today and . . .

75. In my class, the students were being naughty for the substitute teacher. The poor goldfish and parakeet . . .

76. On my way home from school, I was chewing gum and blew the biggest bubble. It . . .

77. My sister forgot to pick me up from school, so I . . .

78. The first time I fly on an airplane, I . . .

79. The first time I saw the tooth fairy, she . . .

80. I was so scared when the biggest tree in the park started talking to me. It said . . .

81. I only wanted to see what was inside the beehive, but . . .

82. Looking at the view from the window of the castle, . . .

83. My favorite vacation was . . .

84. Waking up in the middle of the night, I was startled by the booming sound heard throughout the neighborhood. I . . .

85. Pick a person you admire. Tell why you like him or her.

86. Describe your favorite day, holiday, or birthday.

87. Describe what you love about your favorite season.

88. Love is . . .

89. Friendship means . . .

90. Sharing is . . .

91. Kindness is . . .

92. Happiness is . . .

93. My best friend . . .

94. My dream house . . .

95. Describe your scariest monster . . .

96. Describe your favorite food . . .

97. If I were one inch tall, . . .

98. When I get older, . . .

99. If I were a giant, . . .

100. If I were the teacher for the day, . . .

101. I remember meeting my best friend for the first time . . .

102. If it rained candy, . . .

103. If the whole world were green, . . .

104. I met a visitor from outer space. He/She . . .

105. I never thought I would ever really come across a dragon, but . . .

106. If I won the lottery, . . .

107. If I could change into a . . .

108. Life in Room _____ . . .

109. Describe your no good, very bad day.

110. My favorite TV show sucked me right out of the couch and into its script. I . . .

111. Describe three ways to help others.

112. Describe the steps in playing your favorite game.

113. List the steps in caring for a pet.

114. Write a letter inviting a friend to your Halloween party.

115. Write a letter to your favorite TV show telling the producers why you like it.

116. Write a letter to "Dear Abby."

117. Write directions on how to make a peanut butter and jelly sandwich.

118. Write directions on how to make a cake.

119. Write directions on how to make breakfast.

120. Write directions on how to make your bed.

121. Write directions on how to make a hamburger.

122. Describe the new candy you just developed.

123. Write about your current mayor, including what you like and don't like about him or her.

124. Write about your current governor, including what you like and don't like about him or her.

125. Write about the current president, including what you like and don't like about him or her.

126. Write about your favorite hero, including what you like about him or her.

127. Describe the importance of rain. Be specific.

128. Describe the importance of sun. Be specific.

129. Describe the importance of food. Be specific.

130. Describe the importance of money. Be specific.

131. Use as many details as possible to finish this thought: My sister/brother is a brat. . . .

132. Use as many details as possible to finish this prompt: My room was a mess. . . .

133. Use as many details as possible to finish this prompt: The dragon's physical characteristics were hideous. . . .

134. Use as many details as possible to finish this thought: The math test was difficult. . . .

135. Use as many details as possible to describe this situation: The sand felt good under my toes. The beach . . .

136. Use as many details as possible to finish this prompt: The music was awesome. It . . .

137. Use as many details as possible to complete this thought: They have the best pizza because . . .

138. Using all five of your senses, describe the following: The circus . . .

139. Using all five of your senses, describe the following: A baseball game . . .

140. Using all five of your senses, describe the following: My family's picnic . . .

141. I wonder why . . .

142. What really makes me happy is . . .

143. The most embarrassing day of my life went like this. . . .

144. It is so much fun to _____. First you have to . . .

145. My biggest fear is . . .

146. My dream school . . .

147. My dream class . . .

148. If I were teacher for the day, . . .

149. If I were principal for the day, . . .

150. If I were Martin Luther King, Jr., I would have . . .

151. If I were Cesar Chavez, I would have . . .

152. If I were the president of the United States, I would . . .

153. If I were governor of my state, I would . . .

154. If I were a champion swimmer, I would . . .

155. If I were a champion runner, I would . . .

156. The most frightening thing I ever saw was . . .

157. I remember when I was _____ years old and . . .

158. When I get out of school . . .

159. When I grow up . . .

160. In 20 years, I will be . . .

161. The three most important things I would place in a time capsule this year are _____, _____, and _____ because . . .

162. When I need a safe place to go, I . . .

163. I woke up this morning the size of the Empire State building. I . . .

164. I woke up this morning in the middle of the Civil Rights movement. I . . .

165. I woke up this morning and found myself in a mission. I . . .

166. I woke up this morning and found myself in the year 2100. I . . .

167. My pet dinosaur . . .

168. The day the teacher didn't show up and the principal asked me to fill in as the substitute . . .

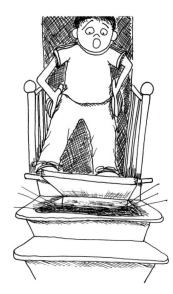

169. If I could turn into anything, I would be . . .

170. If I had three wishes, I . . .

171. If I could make all the rules, . . .

172. Suddenly, my sailboat sprang a leak. I . . .

173. The trapdoor under the stairs always scared me, but I heard a sound like someone screaming and I had to . . .

174. Remember the year when it wouldn't stop raining? For 365 days it rained. We . . .

175. I would use my magic wand to . . .

176. If I could be invisible for one day, I would . . .

177. If I lived in a mansion, . . .

178. If I lived in a jungle, . . .

179. If I lived in the 1920s, . . .

180. If I lived in the 1930s, . . .

181. If I lived in the 1950s, . . .

182. If I lived in the 1960s, . . .

183. If I lived in the 1970s, . . .

184. If I lived in the 1980s, . . .

185. If I lived in the 1990s, . . .

186. If I were a dancer, . . .

187. If I were an airplane pilot, . . .

188. If I were a news anchor, . . .

189. If I were a doctor for children, . . .

190. If I were a painter, . . .

191. If I were a singer, . . .

192. If I were a dentist, . . .

193. In as many details as possible, describe a dream you have had.

194. Describe your dream car.

195. Write three questions you would like to ask a Native American.

196. Write three questions you would like to ask a slave prior to the Civil War.

197. Write three questions you would like to ask a war veteran.

198. Write three questions you would like to ask the president.

199. List all the reasons why people must learn to read.

200. Write about anything you like.

Graphic Writing Organizers

Webbing," or "brainstorming," ideas for writing is one of the oldest strategies for planning an essay, story, friendly letter, or almost any other piece of writing. As children, most of us drew a big circle where we would write our topic. From the center, lines would attach to smaller circles where we would place our ideas around the topic. While this more traditional style is still effective, other useful and productive ways of organizing writing have become popular.

Moving beyond the "web" into graphic organizers that streamline purpose and thought can be much more motivating and purposeful for students. You will find a variety of graphic writing organizers that support a range of genres and writing approaches. These are only a handful. Be creative and tailor them to your themes and writing assignments. Extend beyond the organizer into higher levels of thinking and questioning. Remember that these are organizers. They are tools for students to organizer their thoughts on paper. Choose those that reflect the Common Core Writing Standards your class is working on.

Graphic Writing Organizers: An Overview

Research Organizer

To be used for gathering and organizing research information. The theme and topic might be assigned by the teacher or chosen by the student. Then, related subtopics are noted, followed by notes to use for supporting details. Students will also need to record any sources they used to obtain information about the topic.

Cause-and-Effect Organizer

To be used to explain cause and effect. Students describe a scenario and then explain what occurs given the experience/example.

Hamburger Paragraph Organizer

Begin with the top bun, which is the topic sentence. Each layer between the top and bottom bun is meant to include supporting details. The bottom bun is to serve as a closing sentence or transition sentence for the next paragraph.

Essay Organizer

To be used to organize an essay focused on a particular topic, theme, or prompt. Students open with an outline of the main idea. Then students outline three additional paragraphs to support the main idea. They close with a final paragraph to wrap up the essay.

Web Organizer

To be used when describing a topic using adjectives. Students place the topic/theme in the middle of the spider's body and then list ideas to support the topic in and around the web.

Character Analysis

To be used for organizing experiences about a character from the story. Students write quotes about what a character said, thought, and felt and what actions he or she took.

Venn Diagram

To be used when linking characteristics and attributes. Students use this to show differences and similarities for any two given people, topics, and so forth.

Sense and Feel Organizer

To be used to list words from a story that describes something. The five senses (sight, taste, smell, hear, and touch) as well as what one feels should be considered for writing their descriptive story.

97
Research
Organizer 1
98
Research
Organizer 2

Research Organizers

Research Theme: Dogs

Research Topic: Pugs

Subtopic: Pug History

Notes: Pugs date back to pre-Christian era. Pugs were bred in China and owned by emperors. Dutch traders brought pugs to Holland and England. The breed was recognized in 1885.

Sources: www.pugs.org

Subtopic: Pug Personality

Notes: Pugs are true clowns. They are very loyal to their owners. They are excellent dogs with children. They are eager to please. They love lots of attention.

Sources: J. T. Puggles, *Pugs*, Dog World Publications (2004)

Name: Omar Dominguez   **Research Organizer**
Date: February 4, 2006

Research Theme: _Dogs_
Research Topic: _Pugs_

Pug History
Sub-topic

Notes:
Pugs date back to pre-Christian era.
Owned by Emperors in China.
Bred by the Chinese.
Dutch traders brought pugs to Holland and England.
The breed was recognized in 1885.

Source: www.pugs.org

Pug Personality
Sub-topic

Notes:
Pugs are true clowns.
Pugs are very loyal to their owners.
Pugs are excellent dogs with children.
They are eager to please.
They love lots of attention.

Source: Pugs (2004) Dog World Publications

99
Cause and
Effect
Organizer—
Lower
Grades

Cause and Effect Organizer—Lower Grades

Cause: We watered the plant.
Effect: The plant grew.

Cause: We did not water the plant.
Effect: The plant dried up and died.

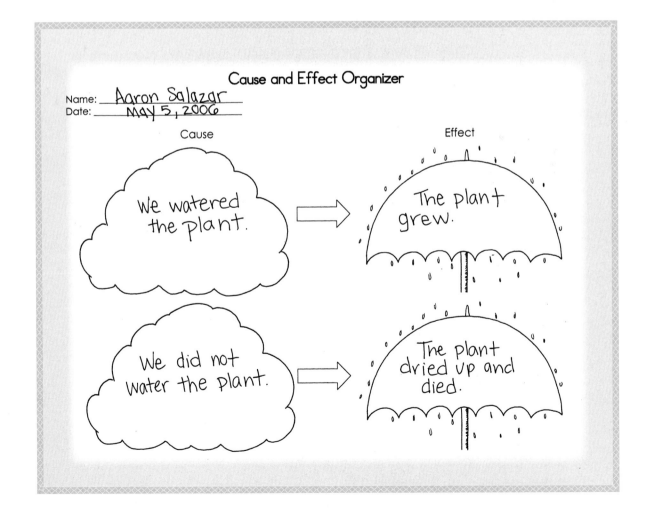

Cause and Effect Organizer

Name: Aaron Salazar
Date: May 5, 2006

Cause | Effect

We watered the plant. → The plant grew.

We did not water the plant. → The plant dried up and died.

100
Cause and
Effect
Organizer—
Upper
Grades

Cause and Effect Organizer—Upper Grades

Cause: We didn't water the plant.
Effect: The plant dried out and died.

Cause: We put the plant in the closet with no light.
Effect: The plant turned yellow and started to die.

Cause: We put the plant in a bag and sealed it.
Effect: The plant withered and started to die.

Cause: We watered the plant and placed it in the sun.
Effect: The plant grew.

Cause and Effect Organizer
Name: Courtney Billet
Date: May 6, 2006

_____ Plant Needs _____
(Title)

Cause | *Effect*

We didn't water the plant.	→	The plant dried out and died.
We put the plant in the closet with no light.	→	The plant turned yellow and started to die.
We put the plant in a bag and sealed it.	→	The plant withered and started to die.
We watered the plant and placed it in the sun.	→	The plant grew.

101

Hamburger
Paragraph
Organizer—
Lower
Grades

Hamburger Paragraph Organizer—Lower Grades

Topic Sentence (top bun):

Charlie is the best brother in the whole world.

Detail Sentences (3 hamburger patties):

Charlie likes to play with me. We play with our toys.

Charlie likes hamburgers, and I do too.

We like to watch cartoons.

Conclusion Sentence (bottom bun):

Charlie is my favorite little brother.

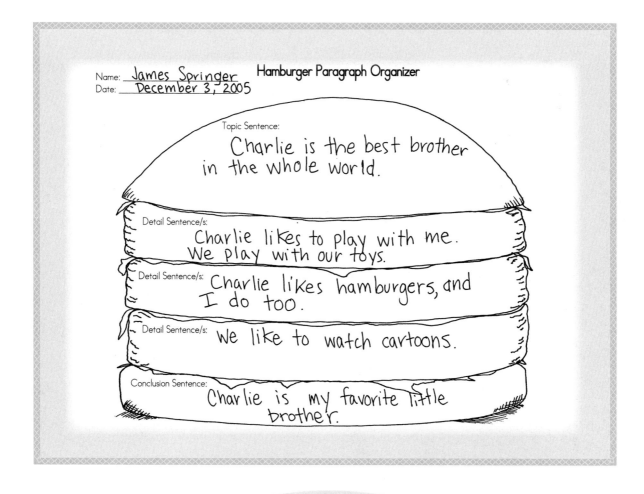

Name: James Springer
Date: December 3, 2005

Hamburger Paragraph Organizer

Topic Sentence:
Charlie is the best brother in the whole world.

Detail Sentence/s:
Charlie likes to play with me. We play with our toys.

Detail Sentence/s: Charlie likes hamburgers, and I do too.

Detail Sentence/s: We like to watch cartoons.

Conclusion Sentence: Charlie is my favorite little brother.

102
Hamburger
Paragraph
Organizer—
Upper
Grades

Hamburger Paragraph Organizer—Upper Grades

Topic Sentence (top bun):

    Pugs are a great breed of dog to own.

Detail Sentences (3 hamburger patties):

    Pugs are a small dog breed. They have flat faces and curly tails.

    Pugs can be very playful and humorous. They also love to cuddle.

    Many years ago monks kept pugs as their companions.

Conclusion Sentence (bottom bun):

    Pugs are truly man's best friend.

Word Bank (drink):

    humorous, playful, cuddly, monks, flat face, curly tail, companion

103
Essay
Organizer

Essay Organizer

Introduction Paragraph

Main idea

Paragraph 1

First point that supports main idea (Evidence/support)

Paragraph 2

Second point that supports main idea (Evidence/support)

Paragraph 3

Third point that supports main idea (Evidence/support)

Closing Paragraph

Wrap it up.

Essay Organizer
Name: *Alexis Jordan*   Date: *March 4, 2015*

Use this organizer to set up your essay. **Essay Topic:** *Narrative*

Introduction Paragraph: Main Idea-*When I was a young girl I became fascinated with triathlons when I watched the stron I had ever seen win her first Ironman triathlon. An Ironman triathlon consists of swimming 2.4 miles, riding a bike for 112 running for 26.2 miles. I know I can't complete an Ironman at my age but I can have that as a goal for the future.*

Paragraph 1:First Point that supports main idea. *Swimming*	Paragraph 2:Second Point that supports main idea. *Biking*	Paragraph 3: Third Point that supports main idea. *Running*
Evidence/Support: *Wetsuit, swimsuit, goggles, swim cap* *I started taking swim lessons when I was a little girl about 6 years old.* *I was in "Tiny Tots" with my older brother as my peer coach because he was a good swimmer.* *I like to swim but I'm not very good at it. I wore yellow floatable arm cuffs until I was 8 years old* *I will need to practice at least 3 times a week if I want to be able to swim for a long distance.*	Evidence/Support: *bike, helmet, tires, tubes, gloves* *My brother also taught me how to ride a bike when I was 7 years old.* *All the kids on the block could ride but I couldn't without my training wheels. I was embarrassed to fall in front of everyone so I never practiced outside on two wheels.* *My brother taught my how to ride on two wheels by having me ride my bike in circles in the garage until I got the hang of it. Then he took me outside when no one was watching.*	Evidence/Support: *shoes, socks, music* *I love to run. I love to run downhill really fast and I like to climb.* *This is my best sport and I know I will be a runner forever.* *I don't know if I will ever want to run a marathon but if I want to do an Ironman someday, I will have to train for one.* *If I could learn to swim as well as I can run, then doing a triathlon will be easier.*

Closing Paragraph: Wrap it up-*Whether or not I ever do an Ironman, I definitely want to complete a triathlon while I am still young. This will give me an idea of what I need to work on the most, even though I know it's swimming. I think if I have enough time to practice all these three sports, I will be a good tri-athlete someday.*

104
Web
Organizer—
Lower
Grades

Web Organizer—Lower Grades

Topic/Idea (spider):

Basketball

Details/Related Ideas (web):

shoes, shorts, basketball, socks, kids, basketball court, referee,
uniforms, points, dribble, jump, hoot, pass, skill, run, basket

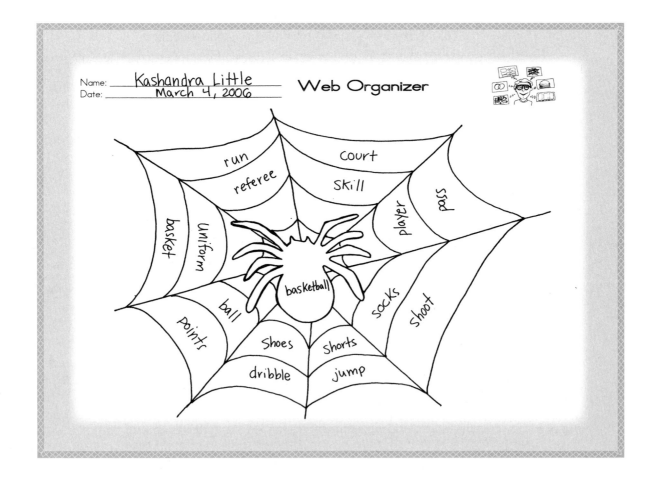

105
Web
Organizer—
Upper
Grades

Web Organizer—Upper Grades

Topic/Idea (spider):

Solar System

Details/Related Ideas (web):

Earth, Sun, Moon, Mercury, Venus, Mars, Jupiter, Saturn, Uranus,
Neptune, Pluto, asteroids, comets, meteorites, stars, planets

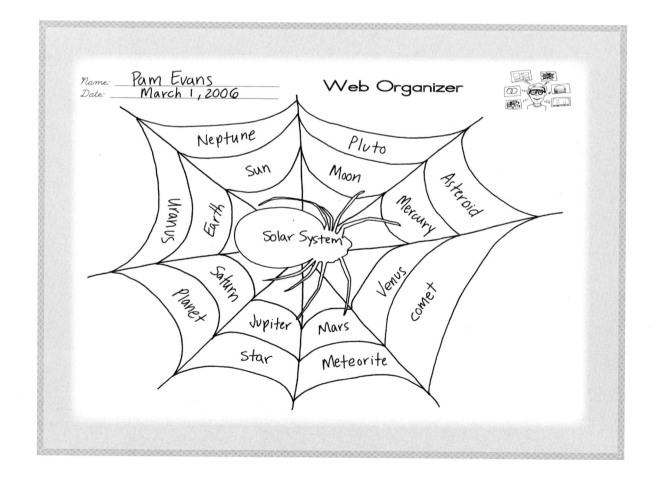

106
Character
Analysis

Character Analysis

Character **Said**

Character **Thought**

Character **Said**

Character **Felt**

Character **Action**

Character **Action**

Character **Action**

Character **Action**

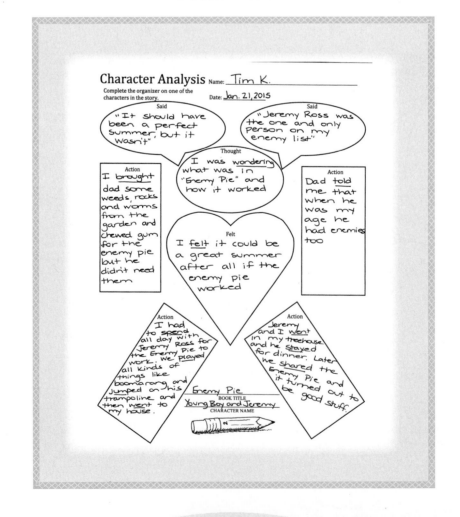

Character Analysis Name: Tim K.

Complete the organizer on one of the characters in the story.

Date: Jan. 21, 2015

Said
"It should have been a perfect summer, but it wasn't"

Said
"Jeremy Ross was the one and only person on my enemy list"

Thought
I was wondering what was in "Enemy Pie" and how it worked

Action
I brought dad some weeds, rocks and worms from the garden and chewed gum for the enemy pie but he didn't need them

Action
Dad told me that when he was my age he had enemies too

Felt
I felt it could be a great summer after all if the enemy pie worked

Action
I had to spend all day with Jeremy Ross for the Enemy Pie to work. We played all kinds of things like boomarang and jumped on his trampoline and then went to my house.

Action
Jeremy and I went in my treehouse and he stayed for dinner. Later he shared the Enemy Pie and it turned out to be good stuff.

Enemy Pie
BOOK TITLE

Young Boy and Jeremy
CHARACTER NAME

107
Venn
Diagram

Venn Diagram

Topics: Dijon, Lamont

Elements in Common: glasses, love books, mom's a teacher, boy

Dijon: lives in a house, rides a scooter, great speller

Lamont: lives in an apartment, likes to mountain bike, fast runner, mathematician

108
Sense and
Feel
Organizer

Sense and Feel Organizer

See: Details about what the writer sees

Taste: Details about what the writer literally or figuratively tastes

Smell: Details about what the writer literally or figuratively smells

Hear: Details about what the writer hears

Touch: Details about what the writer touches/feels with fingers

Feel: Details about what the writer feels emotionally

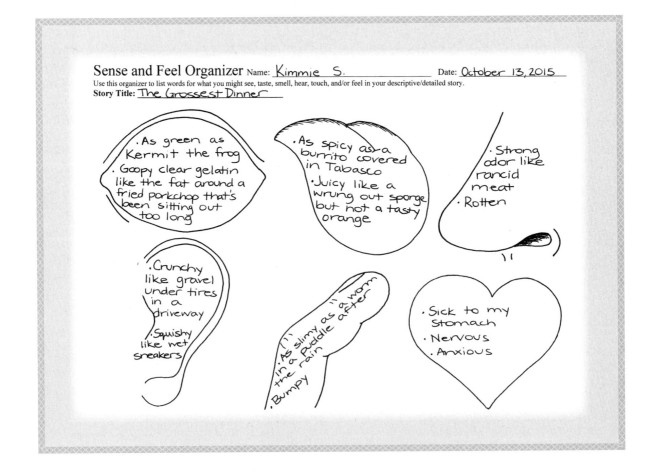

Autobiography Recipe

Materials Needed

Recipe template

Student Guidelines

1. *2–8 Cups of Personality:* Students should introduce themselves by writing two to eight sentences about their personalities. Are they funny? Why? Are they kind and sweet? Are they mischievous? Are they silly? They should use examples of things they do to describe their personalities. The number of sentences depends on the grade level.

2. *1–2 Teaspoons of Future:* In one to two paragraphs, students describe what they would like to do in the future. What do they want to be when they grow up? Why? How will they accomplish this goal? The number of paragraphs depends on the grade level.

3. *1–2 Pints of Interests:* In one to two paragraphs, students will describe their favorite things to do. What interests do they have? What sports do they like to watch or play? What television programs do they enjoy? What types of books do they like to read? What computer games do they play? What activities do they like to do with friends or family? The number of paragraphs depends on the grade level.

4. *1–3 Tablespoons of Family:* Students describe their family life in one to three paragraphs. They should describe what makes their parents, siblings, grandparents, cousins, aunts, and uncles special. The number of paragraphs depends on the grade level.

5. *Mix and Frost with 1 Cup of Conclusion:* When cool, students should add the icing to their recipe by including some finals thoughts about themselves!

6. *Decorate:* Sprinkle the following information onto a cover sheet:

- Self-Portrait
- Name
- Classroom Number
- Teacher Name
- Date

Create a Menu

Think of your favorite type of food (Mexican, Armenian, Italian, Indian, Mediterranean, Southwest). Create a menu for a new restaurant including your favorite menu items from your favorite type of food. This lesson can be related to math, health, and geography.

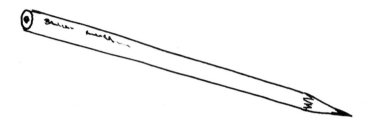

Directions

1. On the front cover, name the restaurant, list the website or e-mail address and phone number, and draw a picture depicting the origin of the type of food your restaurant represents.

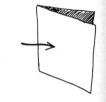

2. On the inside left cover, list the appetizers, salads, soups, and sandwiches along with their prices.

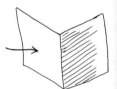

3. On the inside right cover, list the entrees, broken down into meat, seafood, and vegetarian. At the bottom, don't forget to add the side dishes and drinks available. Include prices for all items.

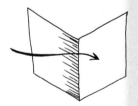

4. On the back cover, give a brief history of the restaurant. Add an explanation of why this restaurant is so good and what diners can expect from their visit to it. Students can also add some historical, cultural, and geographic information about the restaurant's origin.

Create a Newspaper

110
Create a
Newspaper—
Lower Grades

111
Create a
Newspaper—
Upper Grades

Create a newspaper article about a teacher you interview.

Read All About Mr./Mrs./Ms. _____

Interview Questions

1. Why did you want to become a teacher? _____

2. What does your typical day consist of? _____

3. Why do you think teaching is important? _____

4. How does your teaching support the common good in your students? _____

5. Do you have any advice for others who would like to teach? _____

6. What is your favorite part of the job? _____

7. What was your scariest day on the job? _____

8. What keeps you coming back day after day? _____

9. How did you prepare to become a teacher? _____

10. Where do you work? _____

11. Who is your on-the-job mentor? Why? _____

After interviewing your teacher of choice, take the responses to the above questions and create a newspaper article. Don't forget to include a photo, website, and any additional information you have learned about the teacher from other students, staff, or faculty.

Science

This chapter includes activities that can be used at every grade level to grab the students' attention and get them excited about learning science. Have the students use the investigation pages at the beginning of the chapter to track experiments. There are also a handful of templates for students to track their research data to be used for individual explanations or in small groups or for assessment purposes. Included are a science-specific organizer (Science Inventory) and a 4-Step and 6-Step Cycle Organizer for use in teaching about cycles that occur in science, such as life cycles, water cycle, carbon cycle, and so forth.

Consult your state science standards for incorporating these activities into your curriculum,* but consider including some of the Common Core Standards for English Language Arts and Literacy into your planning for science, as many of them overlap across subject areas. The following are some that match well with Science instruction:

As students advance through the grades and master grade level standards in reading, writing, speaking, listening, and language, they are able to exhibit the following as literate individuals:

1. They demonstrate independence.
2. They build strong content knowledge.
3. They respond to the varying demands of audience, task, purpose, and discipline.
4. They comprehend as well as critique.
5. They value evidence.
6. They use technology and digital media strategically and capably.
7. They come to understand other perspectives and cultures.

The CCSs for writing also ask students to organize their data where each grade level is required to complete a variety of tasks including but not limited to the following:

- *Production and Distribution of Writing.* Students respond to questions and suggestions and add details to strengthen writing.
- *Research to Build and Present Knowledge.* Students take notes on sources and sort evidence into categories, conduct research projects, and draw evidence from literary and informational texts to support analysis, reflection, and research.
- *Range of Writing.* Students write over extended times (time for research, reflection, and revision) and shorter time frames (a single sitting or a day or two) for a range of tasks, purposes, and audiences).

*To read the Common Core Standards in more detail and to obtain the grade level specific standards, visit http://www.corestandards.org.

MY INVESTIGATION 1

Experiment:

Scientist:

Date:

Purpose:

Prediction: I predict

Observations:

1.

2.

3.

Conclusion:

MY INVESTIGATION 2

Experiment:

Scientist:

Date:

Purpose:

Prediction: I predict

Observations:

1.

2.

3.

4.

Experiment:

Scientist:

Date:

Observations (continued):

5.

5.

6.

6.

7.

7.

8.

8.

Conclusion:

Draw a picture of your conclusion on a piece of paper.

SCIENCE INVESTIGATION

Experiment:

Scientist:

Date:

Purpose:

Prediction:

Observations:

1.

2.

Experiment:

Scientist:

Date:

Observations (continued):

3.

3.

4.

4.

5.

5.

6.

6.

7.

7.

8.

8.

Science Investigation (2 of 3)

Conclusion:

_____

Illustrate and label your conclusion:

Name: _____

SCIENCE OBSERVATION JOURNAL

Write and illustrate all observations.

Subject: _____ Date: _____ / _____ / _____

Observation: _____

_____

_____

_____

_____

Illustration

Subject: _____ Date: _____ / _____ / _____

Observation: _____

_____

_____

_____

_____

Illustration

Subject: _____ Date: _____ / _____ / _____

Observation: _____

_____

_____

_____

_____

Illustration

115
Science Observation Journal

Name: _____ Date: _____

SCIENCE INVENTORY

Use this organizer to track notes, information, vocabulary, and conclusions from a given chapter/unit.

Unit: _____ Chapter: _____

Section: _____ Pages: _____

☐ Earth ☐ Life ☐ Physical ☐ Environmental

Key Vocabulary (define on back)

1. _____	7. _____
2. _____	8. _____
3. _____	9. _____
4. _____	10. _____
5. _____	11. _____
6. _____	12. _____

Main Idea/s

Concept	Description/Explanation	Illustration
1.		
2.		
3.		
4.		
5.		

4-STEP CYCLE ORGANIZER

Use this organizer to illustrate a cycle that occurs in science, such as life cycles, water cycle, carbon cycle, and so forth. Illustrate and label each step.

6-STEP CYCLE ORGANIZER

Use this organizer to illustrate a cycle that occurs in science, such as life cycles, water cycle, carbon cycle, and so forth. Illustrate and label each step.

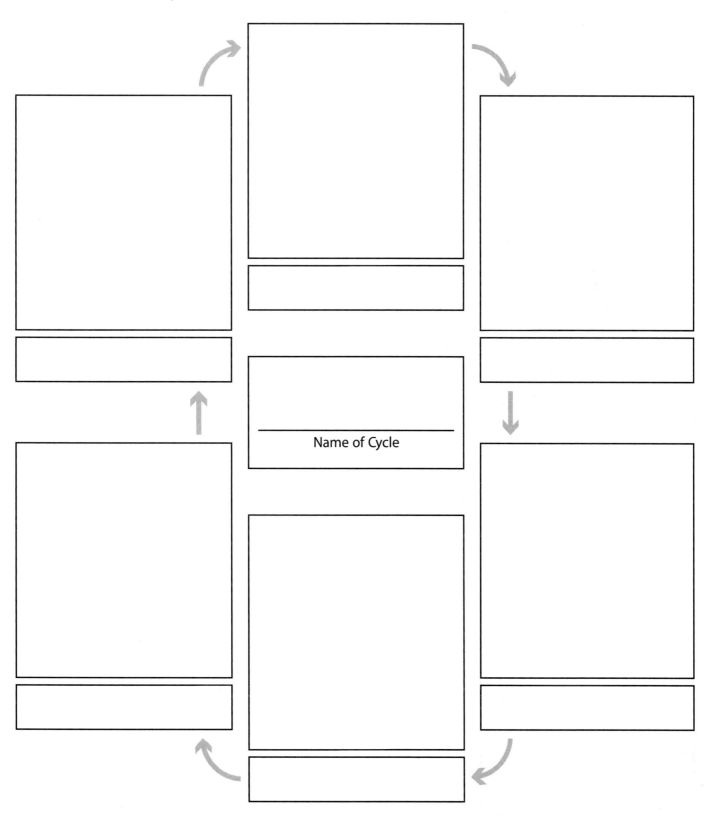

Name of Cycle

Exploring Batteries and Lightbulbs

Simple D batteries and 3V flashlight bulbs can be explored by students to learn about electricity and conduction.

Batteries are a source of electrical energy that can power toys, radios, lightbulbs, and so many more items. In order for electricity to travel, it follows a circuit, or path, from negative to positive. A battery has a negative end and a positive end. Batteries are designed so that the negative particles at the negative end (electrons) cannot travel to the positive end particles (protons). By setting up a complete circuit, or path, the negative particles (charges) can travel to the positive particles (charges) on a path that goes outside of the battery, establishing a current. This results in a complete circuit.

A wire on a lightbulb circuit needs to touch the metal parts of the lightbulb. The metal acts as a conductor. Electrons (negative particles) will not flow through the glass part.

Vocabulary

- positive
- negative
- filament
- terminal
- circuit
- protons
- electrons
- current
- electricity

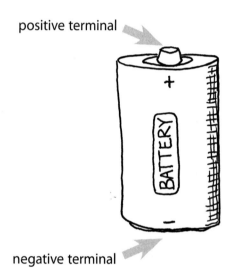

positive terminal

negative terminal

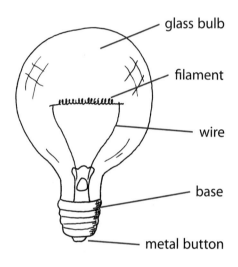

glass bulb

filament

wire

base

metal button

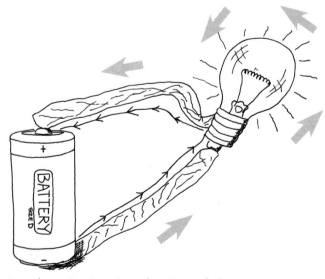

complete circuit using aluminum foil

Explorations

Try different materials as conductors (coins, cotton, paper, etc.).

Try using more than one battery.

Try using several wires/pieces of aluminum foil.

Lightbulbs work because they have a filament wire. The filament is resistant to the flow of electricity. This creates a friction (resistance), so heat is produced as electricity passes through the filament. As the filament heats up, it starts to glow and produce light.

With no bulb or device to receive the electricity, a larger current will build, which is a "short circuit." This can cause the battery to die out more quickly and result in the foil/wire getting warm. In a house a short circuit can be dangerous and sometimes even cause a fire.

Materials

wire

lightbulb

aluminum foil

battery

Steps

1. Light the bulb. Students should be given the lightbulb, battery, and aluminum foil pieces/wire. Allow students through free exploration to try to light the bulb. When does it work? When doesn't it work?
2. Try different variations. Students can try using different items as conductors. Try more than one battery or piece of foil/wire.
3. A complete circuit is formed when the bulb is lit.

Closed circuit = current is flowing

Open circuit = current is not flowing
             (path is interrupted/disconnected)

Hints

- Play around with the materials prior to the lesson. Have alternate conductors for students to use (possibly in baggies). Preparing ahead of time will make your lesson easier.
- Use a flashlight bulb (3V), which can be purchased at your local hardware store.
- Use a D battery.
- When using coins as conductors, use newer, shiny coins. Dull coins won't conduct as well.

Name: _____

Date: _____

Color and label parts of the lightbulb and battery. Draw wires and use arrows to show a circuit.

© McGraw-Hill Education

Making Butter

Making butter is a fun and easy activity. As with any activity of this nature, it is always a good idea to do a test run first to establish what you are comfortable with. You only need heavy whipping cream, which can be found in the dairy section of your grocery store, and a jar with a lid. Students can pair up and shake the cream in a jar. Butter forms within a few minutes (up to 20) and then can be enjoyed. Check with your school or district to be sure it's OK to use these products in the classroom.

How is butter formed? In a nutshell, milk is an emulsion, which is a mixture of two liquids that are not normally mixable. Milk has a fat component (fat soluble) and a protein/carbohydrate component (water soluble). Basically, Mother Nature was creative as milk has fat, carbohydrates, and protein all in one. When whipping cream is churned/shaken for a period of time, most of the water is forced out and the mixture (emulsion) separates. So the fat solidifies and most of the other components are separated out (some skim milk and some buttermilk). The buttermilk can be separated by pouring it off. Then the remaining buttermilk can be washed off the butter in a bowl with cold water. Do this by working the butter with a spoon. As the water turns dark, it can be poured out, thus ridding the butter of excess buttermilk. However, in making small quantities you can just pour off the buttermilk, sample it if you want, and then enjoy the butter. The buttermilk itself can naturally be slightly sour tasting.

Students can discuss how milk and dairy products are made:

1. Grass is eaten by the cow.
2. The cow makes the milk.
3. The cow is milked.
4. The milk is used to make dairy products.

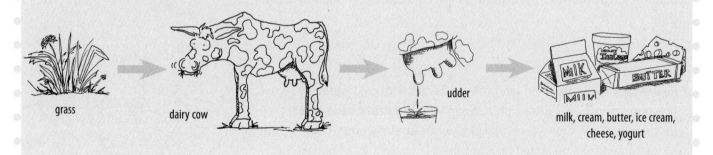

grass   dairy cow   udder   milk, cream, butter, ice cream, cheese, yogurt

Materials

heavy whipping cream

jar with lid (baby food jars work well)

salt

eager shakers

plates

crackers

Steps

1. Open heavy whipping cream: Cream can be used right from the refrigerator or allowed to sit at room temperature for up to 24 hours. Letting the cream sit sours the cream and gives the butter a stronger taste. For this exercise, using the cream from the refrigerator is fine.

2. Add whipping cream to jar: Fill the jar one-third to two-thirds full of the heavy whipping cream. You can add a couple of clean marbles to help churn the butter faster. If marbles are used, you may want to use plastic containers so you avoid breaking a glass jar. Always take precaution with younger students. When you no longer hear the marbles, this usually means they are stuck in the butter and your butter is done. (Marbles are not necessary, but could make an interesting time variable for older students.)

3. Pair students and shake: Shake jar for up to 20 minutes until butter mass is formed. Students can take turns shaking.

4. Pour off the buttermilk: The buttermilk can be sampled. It will have a sour taste.

5. Rinse/wash the butter: You can rinse the butter with cold water. By pressing against the butter with a spoon you squeeze out the excess buttermilk. When the water is darker you can carefully pour it out. A dash of salt to taste can be added to your butter (1 tsp to 1 lb. of butter). Salt helps preserve the butter, but since butter will be eaten, salt is optional. If salt is added, mix it well.

6. Enjoy: Have fun! Have plates with crackers and/or bread for students to sample their butter with.

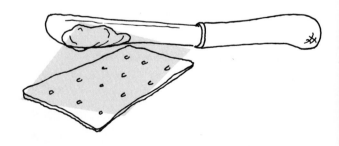

Name: _____

Date: _____

Color and label how dairy products are made. Write about it.

1

_____
_____
_____
_____
_____
_____
_____

2

_____
_____
_____
_____
_____
_____
_____

3

_____
_____
_____
_____
_____
_____
_____

4

MILK

CHOCOLATE IceCream

BUTTER

MIIK

_____
_____
_____
_____
_____
_____
_____

Creating Flubber

Students love making flubber. It is easy and fun! Students observe a change in matter when the ingredients are combined since the resulting substance is a thick goo—like putty. Variations in the recipe can be explored. However, the more liquid it becomes, the more likely it is to stick to clothing. To last longer, the flubber can be stored in a sealed baggie. Color the flubber by adding food coloring to the glue and water part of the mixture.

Materials

bowl
borax
cup
water
glue
2 large jars with lids

Steps

1. Mix borax with water in one jar:
   Mix ¼ cup borax with 4 cups water in one jar.
   Stir until dissolved.

¼ cup borax   4 cups of water

2. Mix glue with water in other jar:
   Mix 1 cup white glue with 1 cup water.
   Tighten jar lid and shake until well mixed.
   Food coloring can be added, if desired.

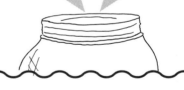

1 cup glue   1 cup water

3. Mix: Pour 1 cup of borax solution into a bowl and add ¼ cup of the glue solution. Knead mixture with fingers.

   The glue mixture will suddenly thicken as it makes contact with the borax solution. Mix quickly to avoid glue bubbles.

1 cup borax solution   ¼ cup glue solution

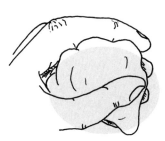

4. Remove flubber, enjoy, and store:
   Once removed, knead to get finished texture. Flubber can be used to make impressions from newspapers and comics. Store in a sealed container or bag.

Explorations

Try varying the ingredients. Try a recipe of:

1 cup cornstarch   1 cup baking soda   ¾ cup water

This mixture creates an amazing "goo" that oozes but will crack when hit with a hammer (hardens when force is applied), only to return to its "goo" state afterward.

Note: Borax can be found with laundry detergents in most grocery stores. It can be toxic if ingested. Please be sure to keep it out of reach of small children and immediately clean up any spills.

Making Ice Cream.

Making ice cream is a hands-on activity that students love. Our culture is a large consumer of ice cream. July is National Ice Cream Month. What better way to teach hands-on math and science concepts than by using something that we all love?

Making ice cream is easy to do. You only need a double zipper-style plastic bag system setup. One larger bag contains ice, and a smaller bag with the ingredients is sealed and inserted inside. The large bag is sealed and shaken, and the cold ice chills the smaller bag and its ingredients, eventually forming ice cream.

Since ice cream recipes and environmental conditions vary, it is a good idea to always try a recipe prior to teaching a lesson

Materials

sandwich-size zipper-style plastic bag
large freezer zipper-style plastic bag
   (thicker and can be reused)
spoons
paper towels
ice
paper cups
rock salt *or* salt
whole milk *or* half-and-half
sugar
vanilla
small plastic cups

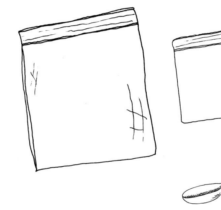

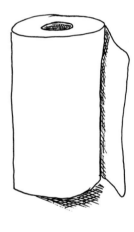

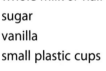

OR

Steps

1. Prepare large bag: Fill large zipper-style freezer bag with ice. You can measure 3 cups if you want students to have measuring practice or simply fill half-full. Add 7 tablespoons salt.

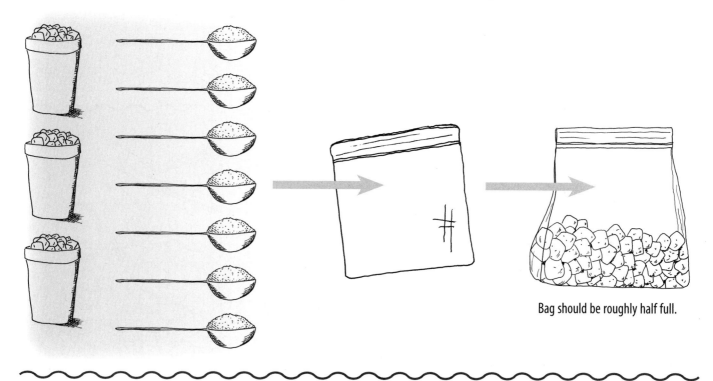

Bag should be roughly half full.

2. Prepare small bag: Add milk (or half-and-half), vanilla, and sugar. Seal bag (squeeze air out and seal tightly). Squish/shake so ingredients are mixed well.

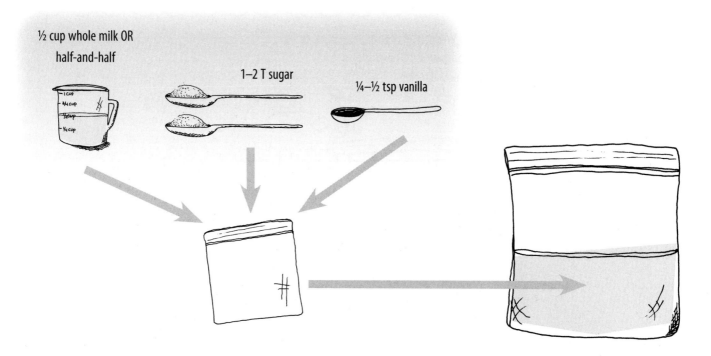

½ cup whole milk OR half-and-half

1–2 T sugar

¼–½ tsp vanilla

3. Insert small bag: Place small sealed bag into larger bag and seal.

4. Shake: Bag can sweat, so shaking outdoors is recommended. You may need to put newspapers down if shaking is done indoors. You can also wrap the bag in a towel or newspaper to avoid getting wet. Shake for about five minutes until mixture becomes ice cream (thick consistency). You can pair students up to share shaking duties.

 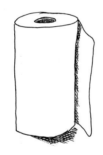 

5. Remove small bag: Remove small bag when ice cream has formed. Wipe the outside of the bag well to remove salt water, which you don't want to mix with the ice cream when the bag is opened.

6. Enjoy the ice cream: Open small bag and serve ice cream. Small plastic cups work well.

Vocabulary

ice cream
milk
sugar
vanilla

Explorations

- Note changes in states of matter for ingredients.
- Note changes in temperature.
- Note changes in weight of ingredients.
- Design alternative preparation methods, for example, replace plastic bags with different containers, use left hand/right hand/both hands to shake, and so on.
- Note time it takes for ice cream to form using alternative methods.
- Try recipe variations such as adding flavors, toppings, and food coloring.

Growing Lima Beans

Lima beans and other seeds can sprout in the classroom, and this germination can be easily observed by students. Lima beans especially are excellent seeds to grow in the classroom because they are large, easily observed, and sprout in only a few days. Seeds have hard exterior "shells" that protect them from drying out until conditions are right for growth. With this experiment, students learn that seeds require certain conditions to grow—water, light, warmth, and oxygen. With these conditions the baby plant (embryo) starts to use the food stored in its seed and will begin to grow. Seeds also grow at different rates. Soaking the seeds overnight can cause them to swell and soften, initiating growth. Soaked lima beans can be opened to observe the embryo inside.

The following is a breakdown of the stages of growth:

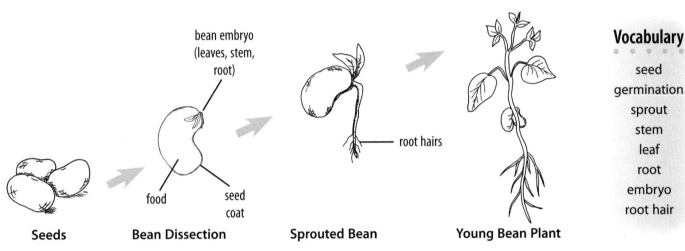

| Seeds | Bean Dissection | Sprouted Bean | Young Bean Plant |

Vocabulary

seed
germination
sprout
stem
leaf
root
embryo
root hair

Explorations

- Predict root and stem growth direction and why.
  - Roots grow down for nutrients and water.
  - Stem/leaves grow up for sun and air.
- Test conditions and observe outcomes.
  - Use different watering solutions (salt, sugar, soda, soap solutions).
  - Use different environmental conditions (cold, hot, dark).
- Try a variety of seeds.
  - Compare germination time.
  - Compare growth rates.
  - Measure stem, leaves, and root.
- Measure daily growth/average daily growth and graph.
- Plant seedlings in soil and continue explorations.

Extension

- Students design their own experiment.
- Create a question to explore. (What would happen if . . . ?)
- Create steps for investigation.
- Test variations and have a control to compare them to.
- Collect quantitative data (number of seeds, number of days, measurements).
- Explain results. Why?
- What would their next experiment be?

Lima Bean Observation

Materials

lima beans
peas and/or radish seeds
  (optional)
small zipper-style plastic
  bag *or* cup
masking tape
permanent marker
water and spray bottle
paper towels

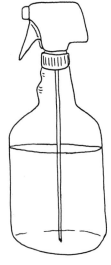

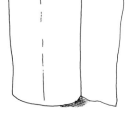

Steps

1. Prepare cup or plastic bag:
   Use either a clear plastic cup or a small zipper-style plastic bag.
   Fold paper towel to fit cup or bag and get it wet so it is damp,
     not dripping.
   Line the cup or bag with the wet paper towel.
   The bag only needs one paper towel.
   If closed properly, you may not even need to water it again.
   Add an additional wadded damp paper towel in the middle
     of the cup to press the lining paper to the edge.

plastic cup

OR

ziplock bag

OR

2. Add seeds:

Slide the seeds, which have been soaked overnight, into the cup or bag between the interior side and the paper towel.

Seal the bag.

Label with masking tape and a permanent marker at top of cup or bag so as not to block the view.

Place the cup on a table near a window if possible. Tape bag to window with seeds facing toward the classroom for observation.

Use one with no water as a variable for students to observe.

Students can conduct the numerous explorations listed or create their own.

Plants can be moved to soil for further observations.

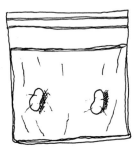

Seed is easily observed through the side of cup/bag and held in place by paper towel. Seeds can also be germinated on damp cotton balls placed in the base of a cup.

3. Observe growth: germination time, root length and direction, stem, leaves, etc. Seeds in the cup, and possibly in the bag, need to be kept moist, not soaking. A spray bottle with a mist setting works well for this. Be careful not to overmoisten—the seeds can mold if they are too wet.

4. Try variations: Other seeds and other plants can be grown.

different seeds

potato suspended in water

carrot top grown in soil

Name: _____

Date: _____

Color and label the parts of a seed and plant.

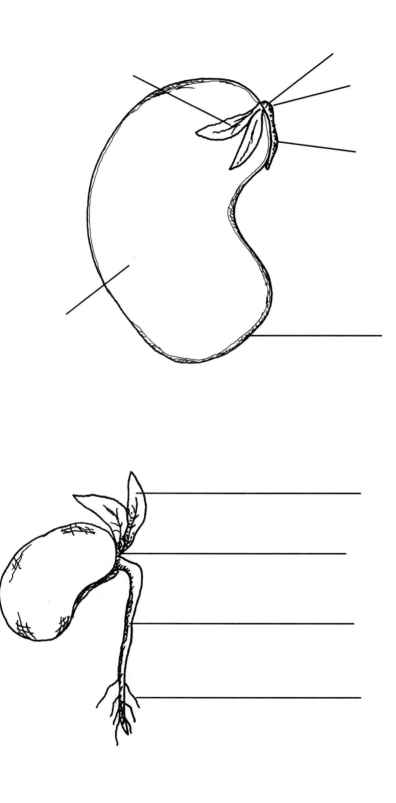

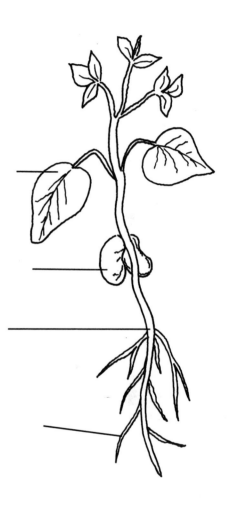

Experimenting with Magnets and Compasses

Magnetism is an important force, and magnets, which vary in strength, are an easy source of free exploration. Students can learn about the force of magnetism and how it is used in a compass. All magnets have a north and south pole. Opposite poles attract (N to S and S to N) and like poles repel (N to N and S to S). Magnets were first discovered as rocks (lodestones) that attracted iron. Lodestones are comprised of magnetite, a mineral that is naturally magnetic. Simple magnets can be made by rubbing a metal object with a magnet in the same direction 10 to 20 times (stronger magnets will make longer lasting magnets).

The biggest magnet of all, earth, has two magnetic poles—north and south. Magnets can be used to create a compass using the attraction of a magnet's poles to those of the earth. A compass is nothing more than a free-spinning magnetic pointer, which will always point north (the south end of the magnetic needle will always rest in the direction of the earth's magnetic pole).

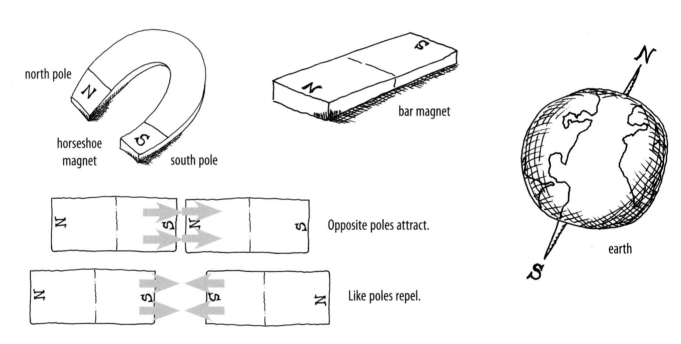

north pole

horseshoe magnet   south pole

bar magnet

Opposite poles attract.

Like poles repel.

earth

Explorations

- Try various objects. What is a magnet attracted to?
- Create magnets by rubbing a metal object against a magnet in one direction 10–20 times.
- Try rubbing it in both directions. What happens?
- Compare magnet strengths. How far can they be from an object to pull it?
- Try rubbing other objects against the magnet. Do they turn into a magnet?
- How could you create a different compass?

Vocabulary

magnet

pole

north

south

lodestone

magnetite

Building a Floating Cork Compass

Materials

cork
cup with water
needle
magnet

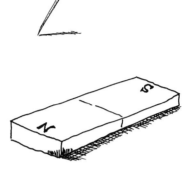

Steps

1. Magnetize the needle:
   Rub the needle 10–20 times
   over the north pole of the
   magnet for its eye to point
   in the same direction.

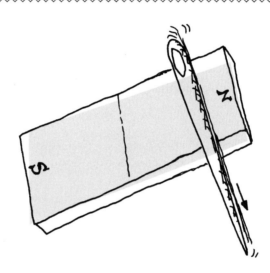

2. Prepare floating cork:
   Slice a small section off the
   cork. Carefully slide the
   needle through the center
   of the cork.

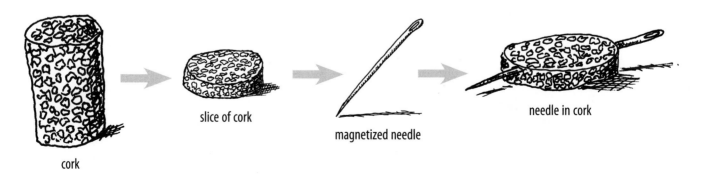

cork

slice of cork

magnetized needle

needle in cork

191

3. Float cork compass in a glass of water: Place cup on a flat surface. Carefully set cork compass in the glass. The needle should lie as parallel to the water as possible. The needle should point north. Determine the direction north and then move the compass and watch it continue to point north.

The magnetized needle will align itself with the earth's magnetic field. Because it is floating it can freely rotate to point north again if the compass is moved.

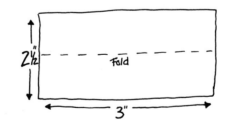

Building a Suspended Needle Compass

Materials

magnet
2 needles
pencil
half an index card
jar
thread

$2\frac{1}{2}''$ Fold

3"

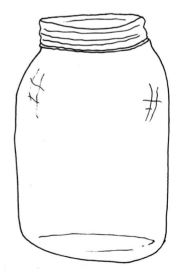

Steps

1. Prepare the index card: Cut an index card in half (2½ inches × 3 inches) and fold one half in half. Thread needle and thread through center.

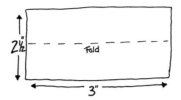

2. Magnetize the two needles: Rub needles over the north end of the magnet (or one end if the north end is not labeled). Rub in *one direction only* 10–20 times from eye to point.

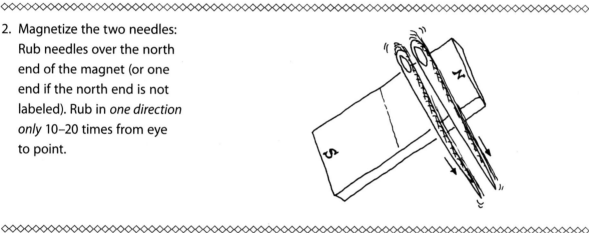

3. Attach needles to inside of index card: Tape needles on each side of the folded half of the index card.

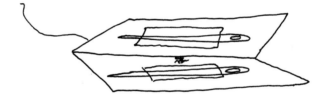

4. Suspend the index card from a pencil into the jar: Suspend from the lip of jar. Make sure card doesn't touch the sides. Hang it approximately 2 inches into the jar. The card will rotate; mark *North* on the end of the card that points north. Try different positions. The card will always point north until the needles lose their magnetism.

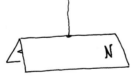
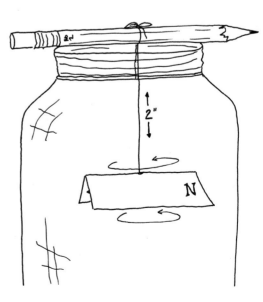

Name: _____

Date: _____

Color (black = north and red = south) and label poles on the magnets and the earth.

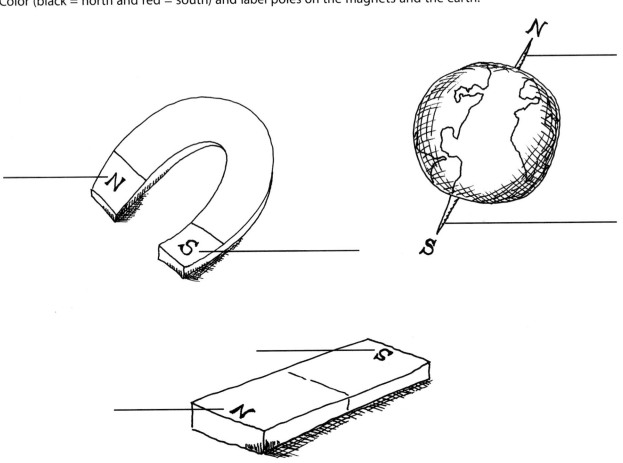

Draw arrows to show the attraction and repulsion of the bar magnet sets.

Label them: Repel or Attract

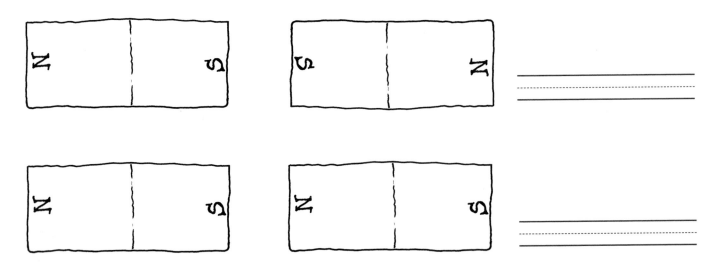

_____

_____

Raising Mealworms

Readily available at your local pet store, mealworms are an excellent opportunity for students to observe a life cycle in the classroom. They aren't really worms at all but larvae. These larvae are the larval stage of the darkling or tenebrio beetle and will molt their outer shell-like coating as they grow (about five times within two months), each time getting larger. The final molt results in the next stage of the cycle, the pupa. The pupa in turn changes into a beetle.

Mealworms can be raised in a plastic tub filled with bran, cornmeal, rolled oats, or cereal flakes, about 1 inch deep. The container should be large and have smooth, steep sides to prevent mealworms from wandering. The container can be left uncovered. A piece of cardboard can provide a good hiding space for the adults. Mealworms will not jump out, bite, or fly (although they have wings, they rarely fly), and they do not smell. Small bits of apple, potato, or carrot can be added as a moisture source once in a while; however, the environment needs to remain dry. A warmer environment (optimal 80°F) and ample moisture sources can help speed up the life cycle, but again the overall environment needs to stay dry. The life cycle takes three to four months, in a colder environment it can take up to five months. Colder environments can possibly suspend the life cycle for an extended period of time.

Mealworm Life Cycle

Egg 7–14 days
Female beetle lays up to 500 eggs in her one to two months of life.

Larvae 30–90 days
Eggs hatch into tiny larvae (mealworms) after two weeks. The larvae eat and grow. Larvae molt, each time expanding and reforming their protective shell coating (about 5 to 12 times in two to three months).

Adult 10–20 days
The pupa changes into the beetle within two to three weeks. The beetle emerges white and darkens to black within a day.

Pupa 10–20 days
When larvae are about 2 cm (¾ inch) long, they go into their final molt. The final molt reveals the pupa stage.

Materials

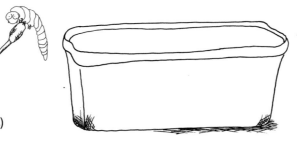

mealworms (larvae)
large plastic container
oatmeal, cornmeal,
   or dry cereal
apple (small piece)
Q-tip (for removal of mealworms)

Steps

1. Set up container: Fill container with about an inch of bedding (oatmeal, cornmeal, or dry cereal).

2. Add mealworms: Larvae can be purchased at a pet store.

3. Maintain habitat: Add a few pieces of fruit for moisture. Include cardboard scraps to hide under. Keep it dry and warm.

4. Observe life cycle.

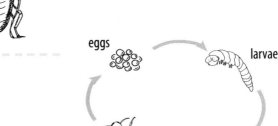

eggs   larvae

adult   pupa

Explorations

- Observe the mealworm (remove with Q-tip).
- How does mealworm react to a flashlight, a wet paper towel, the smell of a Q-tip dipped in peppermint extract, or a gentle blow of air (use a straw)?

Vocabulary

mealworm
larvae
pupa
adult
darkling beetle
life cycle

Name: _____

Date: _____

Color and label the life cycle of a mealworm.

_____
- -

_____
- -

_____
- -

_____
- -

Building Rockets

Building rockets is an exciting way for students to observe a chemical reaction and witness the powerful propulsion forces the resulting gases can have. This classroom rocket uses an empty film canister to house the reaction. Half an Alka-Seltzer tablet and 1 tsp of water are mixed in the sealed canister. The resulting gases build pressure, which creates enough force to propel the canister into the air. Building a rocket around the canister lets students observe how a real rocket would work.

    Students should always be encouraged to ask "What if" questions. What happens if we double the water? Does a change in the amount of water change the launch time needed? Are other containers more effective? Students can change the variables in this activity to explore variations in the experiment. This is a powerful scientific tool that increases understanding through authentic learning.

    It is recommended that students wear protective eyewear and take precaution when launching rockets.

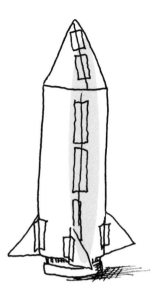

Materials

paper roll
tape
water
Alka-Seltzer
film canister
construction paper

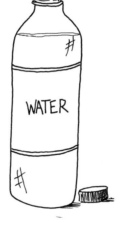

Alternative Ingredients
vinegar
baking soda

198

Steps

1. Cut roll up the middle and slide over the film canister. Tape roll securely to film canister. Tape the tube along the cut seam.

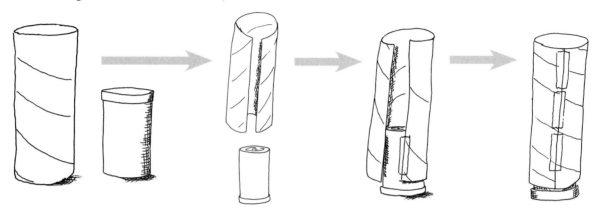

2. Cut into a circle of construction paper. Slide edge of paper over top of other edge to make a cone, and tape along seam. Tape cone to opposite end of tube.

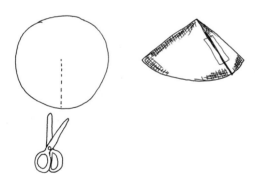

3. Attach three to four fins to the rocket at the base. Be careful not to make it too heavy.

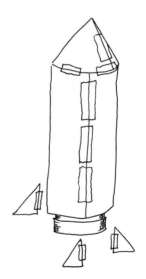

If time is limited, you can launch the canisters without a rocket body. Also you can use an alternative recipe with baking soda and vinegar. Older students can take this and run with it. They can explore all the variations and track distances, heights, and launch times.

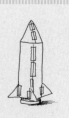

4. Fill rocket and launch outside: Turn rocket upside down and fill canister about one-quarter full of water. Drop in a half tablet of Alka-Seltzer. Immediately close the lid, invert the rocket, and place on the ground. Stand back and wait for the launch. Protective eyewear should be worn.

An alternative to the Alka-Seltzer and water is vinegar and baking soda. The rocket canister lid is packed with baking soda and the canister is filled one-quarter to one-half full of vinegar. Snap the lid on and turn rocket back upright with lid side down. Place on the ground. Stand back.

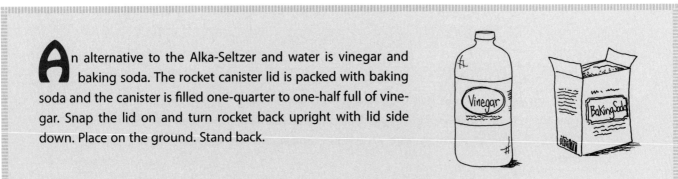

Creating a Volcano

Building volcanoes is an easy way for students to observe a simple chemical reaction and visualize what takes place in a volcanic eruption. This model produces carbon dioxide gas, which builds up and produces an eruption just as the carbon dioxide gas does in a real volcanic eruption.

In an actual volcano, heat deep within the earth's core can cause carbon dioxide gas in magma (hot liquid rock found deep within the core) to expand. This pressure pushes the magma up into vents found in a volcano. The magma then moves up the vents to the earth's surface. The volcano erupts when the magma overflows from the top of the vent and runs down the sides of the volcano. There can be a huge explosion if enough gas has built up and eventually explodes through the surface. Your classroom volcano will demonstrate this explosion on a smaller scale.

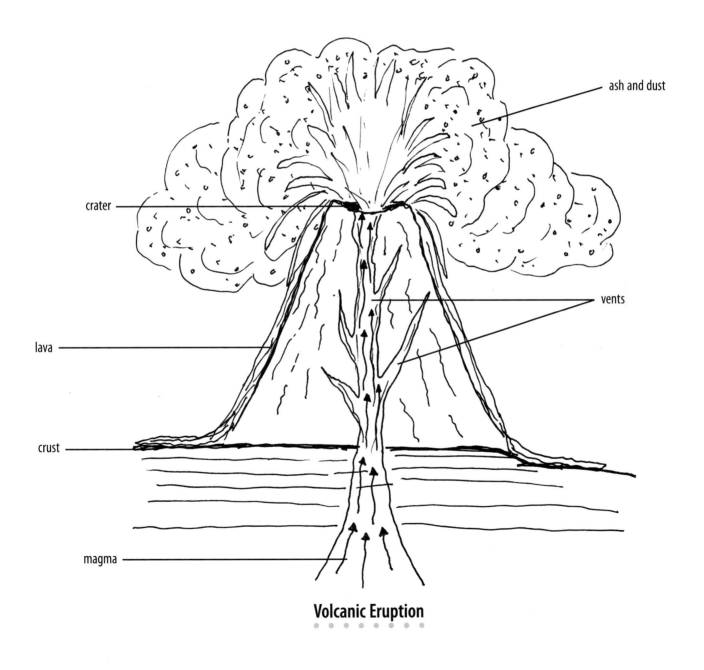

ash and dust

crater

vents

lava

crust

magma

Volcanic Eruption

Materials

dirt *or* salt dough (recipe at right)
pan
plastic water bottle
red food coloring
baking soda
vinegar
liquid detergent

Salt Dough

3 cups flour

1 cup salt

2 T cooking oil

1 cup warm water (more if necessary)

food coloring (optional)

Mix together with hands into a dough.

Steps

1. Build the volcano: Place plastic bottle in a pan. The pan will collect the eruption overflow. Mold the salt dough or dirt around the bottle to build the volcano. Continue working your way up the volcano to the top of the bottle. Leaving the lid on is recommended. Do not cover the top of the bottle with dough.

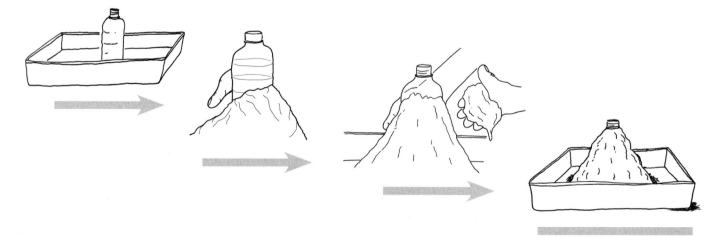

2. Fill the volcano.
   - Fill the bottle almost to the top (⅘) with warm water that has red food coloring added.
   - Add 5–7 drops of liquid detergent.
   - Add 2 T of baking soda using a paper funnel; or put baking soda in tissue paper and drop into the bottle first and then add the other ingredients.
   - When ready, add vinegar to the bottle and watch the eruption of a red foamy mixture quickly rise out of the bottle and flow down the sides of the volcano.

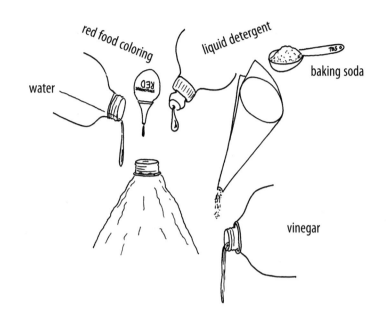

3. Watch the eruption: The baking soda and vinegar create carbon dioxide gas just like a real volcano. This gas causes bubbles to build up and erupt, pushing the liquid in the bottle up, out, and down the sides.

Name: _____

Date: _____

Color and label parts of a volcano. Write about an eruption.

_____

_____

_____

_____

_____

_____

_____

_____

_____

_____

_____

Soda Bottle Terrarium

An excellent hands-on approach to studying the water cycle, life cycle of plants, and closed environments is by building a Soda Bottle Terrarium. Using a two-liter bottle with a cap, some pebbles, soil, seeds, and/or seedlings a simple terrarium can be constructed. It can be studied for a few days or weeks or even throughout the year.

There are several areas of study that can be illustrated by using this simple terrarium environment. Depending on the age of the students, instruction of various aspects of the terrarium can easily be aligned to the Common Core Science Standards. Younger students can easily learn about seed germination and the needs of a plant, and older students can study the water cycle and experiment with variable manipulation of this closed environment.

The Water Cycle

The water cycle is the basically the way water works its way through our environment. There are several phases or stages of the water, or hydrologic, cycle. The phases are transpiration, evaporation, condensation, precipitation, and percolation. All of these can be observed using the terrarium. Here you will find a general overview of the water cycle and its phases.

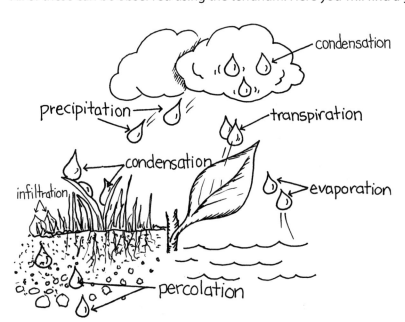

- *Evaporation.* Water vapor rises into the air as water is heated by the sun.
- *Transpiration.* Water vapor rises off of plants.
- *Condensation.* Water changes from vapor back to liquid and collects into clouds or, in this case, on the sides of the terrarium.
- *Precipitation.* Water that condenses becomes heavy and eventually returns to the earth or dirt of the terrarium.
- *Infiltration.* Water passes from the surface of the soil into the soil.
- *Percolation.* Water passes through the soil because of gravity and capillary forces.

Materials

Vocabulary

terrarium
precipitation
condensation
percolation
evaporation
transpiration
germination

empty two-liter soda bottle with lid
scissors
clear packing tape
potting soil
pebbles/stones
seeds (bird seeds, wheat berry, grass, flower, and so forth) or seedlings (can be purchased at a nursery or discount store)
charcoal/moss (optional)

Steps

1. Wash bottle out and remove all labels.

2. CAREFULLY cut off top of bottle about 4–6 inches above the bottom, or just above the bottom line of where the label was.

3. Add small stones, gravel, or pebbles to fill about 1–2 inches of the bottom. This provides an area for extra water to collect.

4. Optional: Add charcoal and moss layer.

5. Add 2–4 inches of potting soil, depending on how high you have cut the base.

6. Add seeds (not too many to avoid overgrowth that terrarium could not support) and/or seedlings.

Adding Charcoal and Moss

- Place activated charcoal/carbon (from a pet store) on top of the pebble/small stone layer to act as a water filter and purifier and to reduce mustiness.
- Spanish or sphagnum moss (commonly found at garden supply centers) can be placed on top of the charcoal or rocks to prevent dirt from settling into the rocks, while still allowing water to pass through. Moss can also serve as decoration on top of the soil and holds in moisture.

7. Add a small amount of water to moisten soil. Do not overwater.

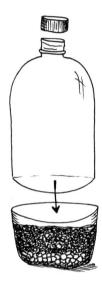

8. Slide top of bottle over base. (If too difficult, a few small cuts from bottom of upper section can be made extending toward top.)

9. Place cap on bottle.

Clear packing tape can be wrapped around the area where the two bottle halves connect. This can prevent the bottle from coming apart and creates a more closed system.

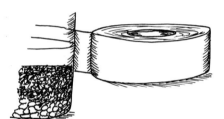

Extensions

- Try potting soil versus soil collected from the area.
- Try sunlight versus no sunlight.
- Plant some seeds near side of bottle to observe germination and plant growth.
- Try a variety of different seeds to track different germination times.

Tips and Recommendations

- Be careful not to overexpose to sun.
- If terrarium is too dry, remove lid and add a small amount of water.
- You should see a small amount water in the rock layer; if it is too wet remove the lid for a period of time, which allows moisture to escape.
- Place terrarium in indirect sunlight; direct sunlight for an extended period of time can create excessive heat in the terrarium and damage plants.

SODA BOTTLE TERRARIUM

Label the terrarium water cycle and write a sentence explaining each phase. Color each water droplet blue.

Word Bank: evaporation transpiration condensation precipitation infiltration percolation

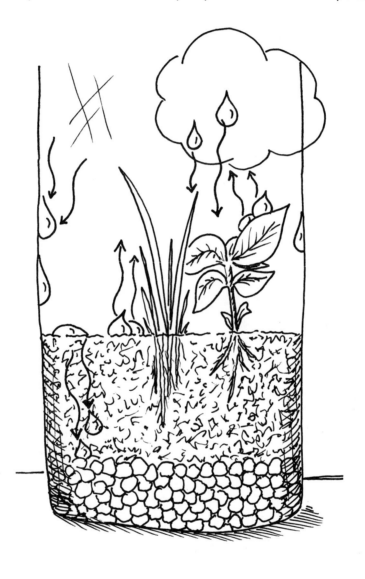

_____

_____

_____

_____

_____

Science Picture Books

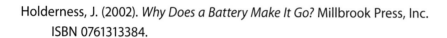

Batteries

Flaherty, M. (2004). *Electricity and Batteries.* Stargazer Books. ISBN 1932799680.

Gardner, R. (2004). *Electricity and Magnetism: Science Fair Projects Using Batteries, Balloons, and Other Hair-Raising Stuff.* Enslow Publishers, Inc. ISBN 0766021270.

Holderness, J. (2002). *Why Does a Battery Make It Go?* Millbrook Press, Inc. ISBN 0761313384.

Still, D. (2004). *Electricity: Bulbs, Batteries, and Sparks.* Picture Window Books. ISBN 1404802452.

Stillinger, D. (2003). *Battery Science.* Klutz Publishing. ISBN 159174251X.

Butter

Cool, J. (2003). *Toast: 60 Ways to Butter Your Bread and Then Some.* Chronicle Books LLE. ISBN 081185553.

Erlback, A. (1995). *Peanut Butter.* Lerner Publishing Group. ISBN 0822597098.

Lindman, M. (1995). *Snipp, Snapp, Snurr and the Buttered Bread.* Albert Whitman. ISBN 0807574910.

Ralph, J., R. Gompf (1995). *Peanut Butter Cookbook for Kids.* Vol. 1. Hyperion. ISBN 0786810289.

Wake, S. (1990). *Butter.* Lerber Publishing Group. ISBN 087614427X.

Flubber

Blakey, N. (1996). *Lotions, Potions, and Slime.* Ten Speed Press. ISBN 188367221X.

Elder, V. (1997). *Flubber: My Story.* Disney Press. ISBN 0786842008.

Kline, S. (1989). *Horrible Harry and the Green Slime.* Viking. ISBN 0670824682.

Seuss, Dr. (1976). *Bartholomew and the Oobleck.* Random House, Inc. ISBN 0394800753.

Sneider, C. (1998). *Oobleck: What Do Scientists Do?* University of California, Berkeley, Lawrence Hall of Science. ISBN 0924886099.

Ice Cream

Daly, K. (2005). *The Good Humor Man.* Golden Books. ISBN 0375832807.

Greenstein, E. (2003). *Ice Cream Cones for Sale!* Scholastic, Inc. ISBN 0439327288.

Henkes, K. (2003). *Wemberly's Ice-Cream Star.* HarperCollins Children's Books. ISBN 0060504056.

Snyder, I. (2003). *Milk to Ice Cream.* Children's Press. ISBN 0516242687.

Taus-Bolstad, S. (2003). *From Milk to Ice Cream: Start to Finish Series.* Lerner Publishing Group. ISBN 0822507145.

Lima Beans

Carle, E. *The Tiny Seed.* Simon & Schuster Children's. ISBN 088708155X.

Jordan, H. (1992). *How a Seed Grows.* HarperCollins Children's Books. ISBN 0064451070.

Rockwell, A. (1999). *One Bean.* Walker and Company. ISBN 0802775721.

Saunders-Smith, G. (1997). *Beans.* Capstone Press. ISBN 1560654872.

Worth, B. (2001). *Oh Say Can You Seed? All About Flowering Plants.* Random House, Inc. ISBN 0375810951.

Magnets and Compasses

Branley, F. (1996). *What Makes a Magnet?* HarperCollins Children's Books. ISBN 0064451488.

Carmi, R. (2002). *Amazing Magnetism.* Scholastic, Inc. ISBN 0439314321.

Lauw, D., & Puay, L. (2001). *Magnets.* Crabtree Publishing Co. ISBN 0778706095.

Rosinsky, N. (2002). *Magnets: Pulling Together, Pushing Apart.* Picture Window Books. ISBN 140480014X.

Schreiber, A. (2003). *Magnets.* Penguin Young Readers Group. ISBN 0448431491.

Mealworms

Carle, E. (1994). *The Very Hungry Caterpillar.* Penguin Young Readers Group. ISBN 0399226901.

Himmelman, J. (2001). *Mealworm's Life.* Scholastic Library Publishing. ISBN 0516272861.

Mason, A. (2001). *Mealworms: Raise Them, Watch Them, See Them Change.* Kids Can Press, LTD. ISBN 1550745069.

Rockwell, T. (1977). *How to Eat Fried Worms.* Scholastic Library Publishing. ISBN 0531026310.

Schaffer, D. (1999). *Mealworms.* Capstone Press. ISBN 0736802096.

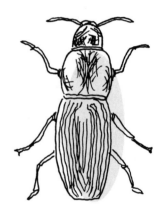

Rockets

Bredeson, C. (2003). *Lift Off!* Scholastic, Inc. ISBN 0516269542.

Mitton, T. (2000). *Roaring Rockets.* Houghton Mifflin, Co. ISBN 0753453053.

Richardson, H. (2001). *How to Build a Rocket.* Scholastic Library Publishing. ISBN 0531139980.

Scholastic, Inc. (2004). *I Spy a Rocket Ship.* Scholastic, Inc. ISBN 043945526X.

Wallace, K. (2001). *DK Readers: Rockets and Spaceships.* DK Publishing, Inc. ISBN 0789473593.

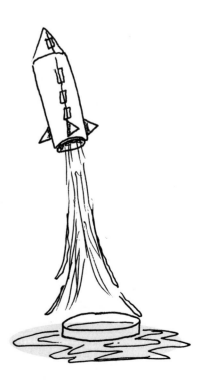

Volcanoes

Herman, G. (1996). *The Magic School Bus Blows Its Top.* Scholastic, Inc. ISBN 0590508350.

Moores, E. (2003). *Volcanoes and Earthquakes.* Barnes and Noble Books. ISBN 0760750734.

Simon, S. (2002). *Danger! Volcanoes.* North-South Books. ISBN 1587171813.

Stamper, J. (2003). *Voyage to the Volcano.* Scholastic, Inc. ISBN 0439429358.

Wood, L. (2001). *Volcanoes.* Scholastic, Inc. ISBN 0439295858.

Water Cycle

Frost, H. (2000). *The Water Cycle.* Pebble Books. ISBN-13 9780736848749.

Hammersmith, C. (2011). *The Water Cycle.* Capstone Press. ISBN-13 9781429671422.

Harman, R. (2005). *The Water Cycle: Evaporation, Condensation and Erosion.* Heinemann Educational Books. ISBN-13 9781403470669.

Koontz, R. (2011). *Water Goes Round: The Water Cycle.* Capstone Press. ISBN-13 9781429662314.

Olien, R. (2005). *The Water Cycle.* Capstone Press. ISBN-13 9780736851824.

Social Science

This chapter contains ideas and tools for creating a variety of writings related to social science. Types of writings include cultural reports, state and country reports, and careers in the community reports. Guidelines for developing autobiographical reports are provided, along with a variety of other meaningful social studies–related organizers. For example the Social Studies Inventory can be used when starting a new chapter or unit, and the time lines can be helpful when looking at the life of a historical event or person of significance.

Consult your state social science standards for imbedding these activities into your curriculum,* but consider including some of the Common Core Standards for English Language Arts and Literacy into your planning for Social Science. Many of them overlap across subject areas. The following are some that match well with Social Science instruction.

The CCSs for writing asks students to organize their data where each grade level is required to complete a variety of tasks including but not limited to the following:

- *Production and Distribution of Writing.* Students respond to questions and suggestions and add details to strengthen writing.
- *Research to Build and Present Knowledge.* Students take notes on sources, sort evidence into categories, conduct research projects, and draw evidence from literary and informational texts to support analysis, reflection, and research.
- *Range of Writing.* Students write over extended times (time for research, reflection, and revision) and shorter time frames (a single sitting or a day or two) for a range of tasks, purposes, and audiences.

---

*To read the Common Core Standards in more detail and to obtain the grade level specific standards, visit http://www.corestandards.org.

Name: _____ Date: _____

SOCIAL STUDIES INVENTORY

Use this organizer to track your notes on a historical figure or event from a given chapter/unit.

Unit: _____ Section: _____

<table>
<tr><td colspan="2">Key Vocabulary (define on back)</td><td colspan="2">Summary</td></tr>
<tr><td>1. _____</td><td>7. _____</td><td colspan="2"></td></tr>
<tr><td>2. _____</td><td>8. _____</td><td colspan="2"></td></tr>
<tr><td>3. _____</td><td>9. _____</td><td colspan="2">Time Line</td></tr>
<tr><td>4. _____</td><td>10. _____</td><td colspan="2">Date</td></tr>
<tr><td>5. _____</td><td>11. _____</td><td colspan="2"></td></tr>
<tr><td>6. _____</td><td>12. _____</td><td colspan="2">Event</td></tr>
</table>

Event/Historical Figure (date and name)	Description (Write a brief description.)	Significance (State the historical significance.)
1.		
2.		
3.		
4.		

Overall Significance

Name: _____ Date: _____

TIME LINE ORGANIZER 1

Use this time line to organize events chronologically. Include the times and a description of the events.

Time/Date	Event
	_____ _____ _____ _____
	_____ _____ _____ _____
	_____ _____ _____ _____
	_____ _____ _____

TIME LINE ORGANIZER 2

Use this time line to organize events chronologically. Include the times and a description of the events.

Time/Date	Event

Heritage Report

Grades 3–6

Sample Cover

A heritage report is an excellent opportunity for students to investigate their own family backgrounds. Students will create a family tree and write about their family. They will also select an older relative to interview for the final part of this report. These reports can be shared and displayed to celebrate the diversity and multiculturalism that exists in our nation.

Students will begin by collecting family pictures. They need a photo of themselves, one of their family, and one of an older relative to be interviewed. Additional photos of extended family members and their immediate family can be used on a photo collage report cover (8½" × 11").

Students will create a family tree using the template provided or create their own. The class can establish how far back and out the tree should extend. A simple family tree may only trace back to the grandparents and out to uncles and aunts. A more advanced tree may include great-grandparents and cousins. Using the leaf bunches, students need to label each bunch with the relative's name and relationship to them and then draw an illustration or add a photo. Students can have their parents or guardians help them with this assignment. The family tree will become the second page of the report.

Students will then start their report by writing a short narrative about themselves. The personal data sheet can assist them in gathering and organizing their personal information. Students will describe who they are, including what they like to do, what they like or dislike about school, and what they like or dislike about home. They will also select and describe up to four family members who are special to them. This narrative should be two to four paragraphs.

Next students will introduce the family member they have selected to interview. Essentially, the student will be writing a biography of that person. Using the interview checklist as a guide and adding any additional questions that are applicable, students will ask their selected person about his or her life. Students will ask their interviewees to describe some significant experiences of their childhood, adolescence, and adulthood. Students can call or visit this family member for the interview.

As part of the interview process, students will record the questions and answers. For their final report, students will combine the questions and answers from the interview into a written essay describing the person.

Heritage Report Outline

1. One paragraph: brief personal narrative (personal photo)
2. Two to four paragraphs: family member descriptions (family photo)
3. One paragraph: introduction of family member to be interviewed (relative photo)
4. Two to four paragraphs: biography of interviewed relative

Sample Family Tree

HERITAGE REPORT

BY

_____

CREATE A FAMILY TREE 1

1. Use a leaf bunch for each family member or create your own.

2. Write the family member's name and relationship to you on each bunch.

3. Draw or glue a picture of that person above his or her name.

4. Use additional leaf bunches to fill in your tree.

CREATE A FAMILY TREE 2

1. Use a leaf bunch for each family member or create your own.

2. Write the family member's name and relationship to you on each bunch.

3. Draw or glue a picture of that person above his or her name.

4. Use additional leaf bunches to fill in your tree.

132
Family Tree: Trunk and Limbs

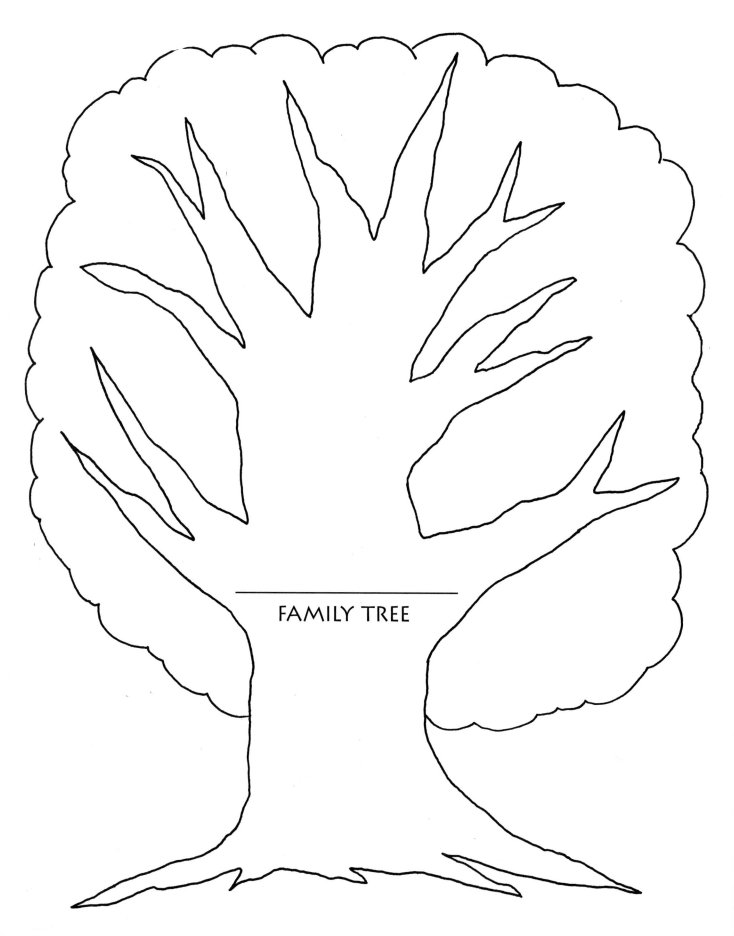

FAMILY TREE

PERSONAL DATA SHEET

Complete the data sheet and use as a guide for writing your report.

Name: _____ Birthday: _____

Address: _____ _____ house _____ apartment _____ condo

Hobbies/Interests: _____ Pets: _____

_____ Favorite Foods: _____

_____ Favorite Music: _____

_____ Favorite TV Show: _____

_____ Favorite Movie: _____

Family Data: _____ mother _____ father _____ guardian _____ brothers _____ sisters _____ cousins

_____ grandfathers _____ grandmothers _____ uncles _____ aunts

FAMILY MEMBER PROFILES

(Profile up to four family members. Choose relatives who are important to you. Write up to four things/memories about the person that show why he or she is special.)

Relative's name: _____ Relative's name: _____

Relationship: _____ Relationship: _____

_____ _____

_____ _____

_____ _____

_____ _____

Relative's name: _____ Relative's name: _____

Relationship: _____ Relationship: _____

_____ _____

_____ _____

_____ _____

_____ _____

Interview: Name: _____ Relationship: _____

INTERVIEW CHECKLIST GUIDE

Name: _____

Relation: _____

Date of Birth: _____

Birth Place: _____

Nationality: _____

> photo/illustration

Childhood (describe any significant experience)

☐ location: _____

☐ _____ brothers and _____ sisters

☐ parents/guardian: _____

☐ home: Did you live in a house, in an apartment, on a farm?

☐ food: What foods did you eat? What traditional foods did you eat?

☐ games/play/sports: Were you involved in sports? What games did you play? With whom?

☐ awards/honors/accomplishments: Did you win any awards or receive special recognition?

☐ school: Did you attend school? How far did you get in your studies? Degrees?

☐ pets: Did you have any family pets? What were they?

☐ work: Did you work as a child or a teenager? What jobs did you have?

Adulthood

☐ location: Where have you lived as an adult?

☐ school: Did you attend a college, university, or technical school?

☐ military: Did you serve in the military? Which branch? Did you ever fight in a war? Describe.

☐ work: What is/was your trade or profession?

☐ marriage: When did you meet? Describe your life together.

☐ home: Where do you live now? Describe your home/s.

☐ other: Are there any other significant experiences you would like to share about your life?

INTERVIEW CHECKLIST RECORD

Name: _____

Relation: _____

Date of Birth: _____

Birth Place: _____

Nationality: _____

photo/illustration

Childhood

☐ location: _____

☐ _____ brothers and _____ sisters

☐ parents/guardian: _____

☐ home: _____

☐ food: _____

☐ games/play/sports: _____

☐ awards/honors/accomplishments: _____

☐ school: _____

☐ pets: _____

☐ work: _____

Adulthood

☐ location: _____

☐ school: _____

☐ military: _____

☐ work: _____

☐ marriage: _____

☐ home: _____

☐ other: _____

Historical Figure/Event Report
Grades 2–6

A report on a historical figure or event is an excellent chance for students to improve their research skills and learn about U.S. history. Students will choose an important person (Martin Luther King, Jr., Cesar Chavez, Rosa Parks, Bill Clinton, etc.) or event (e.g., the Civil Rights movement, the Underground Railroad, the death of a U.S. President) to research. In making their choice it is important to be realistic. Students need to make sure they will have access to books, magazines, newspapers, and the Internet to help guide their research. Students should look for these resources before they choose their person or event.

The guidelines provided in this section will help students organize their ideas and information and assist them in writing complete research reports. Students can start their research with a traditional KWL organizer, which will guide their research. Students will explore the background/history leading up to the event or person's accomplishments. Next they will research the cause of the event/accomplishment, what brought it about, or what influenced it. They will explain the specific examples that influenced the event or person. Then students will discuss the historical impact of this person or event. In conclusion, they will write about the personal impact that the event or person has had on their lives, if applicable.

To accompany their report, students will create a time line of the history surrounding the person/event. This will include events leading up to, during, and following the event or accomplishment. Students can summarize and illustrate these events on their time line. Several time line templates can be glued together if needed, or students may wish to create their own time lines.

Finally, students can make a cover page illustrating their important historical figure or event.

Report Outline

1. One to two paragraphs: introduction of important person or event

2. Three to six paragraphs: background, cause, influences, and effects

3. One paragraph: personal impact and insights

Name: _____ Date: _____

HISTORICAL EVENT ORGANIZER

Use this organizer to write about a historical event that you are studying.
Illustrate a "snapshot" of the event, and answer questions pertaining to the event.

Event: _____

Caption:

When? When did the event occur? What was the political/social/economic climate?

Who? Who was present, involved, or participated?

Where? Where did the event occur? What was the significance of the location?

What? What took place?

Why? Why did this happen?

How? How did this event affect our history? Is there an impact on your life today?

Use the back of this page to write about the significance of this event and the possible outcomes had it not occurred.

The following is an overview of the historical figure/event report.

HISTORICAL FIGURE/EVENT REPORT OVERVIEW

Name of Figure/Event: _____

Personal Importance/Significance (Why are you interested in this person/event? Give examples.)

_____

KNOW—What do I know? (Why I am interested in this. What does this mean to me?)

_____

WANT—What do I want to know more about? (Give examples.)

_____

LEARNED—What have I learned through this report? (Conclusion: Have you gained more respect? Were there any surprises? Give examples.)

_____

BACKGROUND HISTORY—What led up to the event/person's accomplishment/s? When did the vision/inspiration begin?

_____

CAUSE—How did the event or accomplishment come about? What events inspired this? What people influenced this?

_____

INFLUENCES—Who or what circumstances had a major influence on this person or event? What role did parents/family/community play?

_____

EFFECT—What impact on history has this person or event had?

_____

Name: _____ Date: _____

HISTORICAL FIGURE/EVENT REPORT

Name of Figure/Event: _____

Personal Importance/Significance (Why are you interested in this person/event? Give examples.)

_____

_____

_____

_____

KNOW—What do I know? (Why I am interested in this. What does this mean to me?)

_____

_____

_____

_____

WANT—What do I want to know more about? (Give examples.)

_____

_____

_____

_____

LEARNED—What have I learned through this report? (Conclusion: Have you gained more respect? Were there any surprises? Give examples.)

_____

_____

_____

_____

HISTORICAL FIGURE/EVENT REPORT

BACKGROUND HISTORY—What led up to the event/person's accomplishment/s? When did the vision/ inspiration begin?

____

____

____

____

CAUSE—How did the event or accomplishment come about? What events inspired this? What people influenced this?

____

____

____

____

INFLUENCES—Who or what circumstances had a major influence on this person or event? What role did their parents/family/community play?

____

____

____

____

EFFECT—What impact on history has this person or event had?

____

____

____

____

HISTORICAL FIGURE/EVENT TIME LINE

Write about the significant events leading up to, during, and following the event or person's accomplishments. Record the date for each item, briefly summarize, and illustrate. Attach an additional time line if needed.

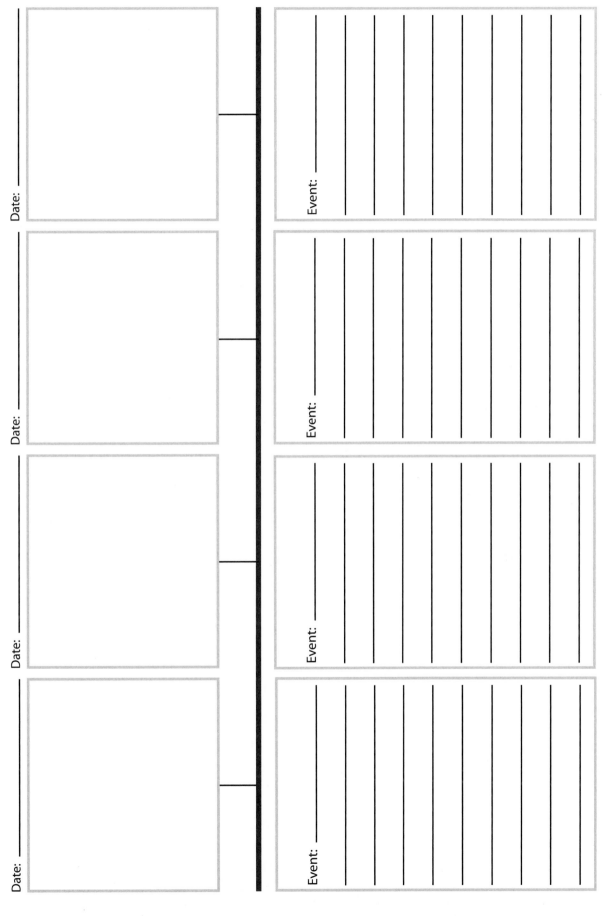

Date: _____

Date: _____

Date: _____

Date: _____

Event: _____

Event: _____

Event: _____

Event: _____

Personal and Cultural Report
Grades 4–6

A personal and cultural report is an excellent opportunity for students to explore their own culture and gain an appreciation for who they are. It is also an opportunity to explore their views on multiculturalism and to learn to appreciate other cultures. Using a large (9 × 12) manila envelope that is cut open along the side edges (*not* the bottom), students can create a personal/cultural report that is unique and personal. Photographs are used, and it is recommended that these images be scanned or copies made of the originals, if possible. Students can use the personal and cultural report breakdown page to assist them in organizing their thoughts and information. The following is an overview of the complete report.

Report Outline

1. Front: 1–2 paragraphs—personal narrative
2. Inside Top: 1–2 paragraphs—family description/culture
3. Inside Bottom: 1–2 paragraphs—ancestor biography/connection
4. Back: 1–2 paragraphs—multicultural views/experiences

FRONT

- Teacher's Name
- Room Number
- Student Name
- Photo
- Any Other Information

Student Photo

Under the photo students should describe:

☐ Who they are
☐ Where they were born
☐ Who raised them
☐ What their position is in their (nuclear and extended) family
☐ What special abilities and interests they have
☐ How they feel about school and learning

INSIDE TOP

Family Photo (in a favorite context if possible)
Under the photo students should describe:

☐ Who their family is

☐ Where they were born or raised

☐ What special interests they share as a family

☐ What beliefs are held regarding culture and cultural diversity

☐ What overall feelings and/or conversations take place in their home about culture and cultural diversity

INSIDE BOTTOM

Ancestor's Photo
Under the photo students should describe:

☐ Relative's culture

☐ Relative's background

☐ Which side they know more about: mother's or father's and why

☐ How children are raised in their culture

☐ What they treasure from their grandparents

☐ What values they want to pass down to their children and family members one or two generations in the future.

☐ Any special memories, celebrations, or family gatherings (Explain in detail.)

BACK

• • •

Students should describe:

☐ What experiences they have had with diversity and cultures other than their own

☐ What languages they have learned (how and to what extent)

☐ Any travel to another country (where, and what they experienced)

☐ What multicultural education means to them

☐ What they have studied

☐ What knowledge and experience they have about people who are English learners and/or culturally different from themselves

☐ How they treat people from a different culture

☐ Examples of times they have befriended a person of a different cultural background

PERSONAL AND CULTURAL REPORT CHECKLIST

FRONT

- ☐ Teacher's Name
- ☐ Room Number
- ☐ Your Name
- ☐ Photo
- ☐ Any Other Information

Under Your Photo:

- ☐ Describe yourself.
- ☐ Who are you?
- ☐ Where were you born?
- ☐ Who raised you?
- ☐ What is your position in your (nuclear and extended) family?
- ☐ What special abilities and interests do you have?
- ☐ How do you feel about school and learning?

BACK

- ☐ Describe what experiences you have had with diversity and cultures other than your own.
- ☐ What languages have you learned (how and to what extent)?
- ☐ Have you traveled to another country? If so, where? What did you experience?
- ☐ Describe what multicultural education means to you.
- ☐ What have you studied?
- ☐ What is your knowledge and experience about people who are English learners and/or culturally different from you?
- ☐ How do you treat people from a different culture?
- ☐ Give examples of times you have befriended a person of a different cultural background.

INSIDE TOP

Family Photo (in a favorite context if possible, as it will help the teacher get to know you sooner)

Under the Photo:

- ☐ Describe your family members.
- ☐ Who are they?
- ☐ Where were they born or raised?
- ☐ What special interests do you share as a family?
- ☐ What are you being raised to believe regarding culture and cultural diversity?
- ☐ What are the overall feelings and/or conversations in your home about culture and cultural diversity?

INSIDE BOTTOM

Ancestor's Photo

Under the Photo:

- ☐ What was his or her culture?
- ☐ How much do you know about your own background?
- ☐ Do you know more about your father's side of the family or your mother's? Or neither?
- ☐ Why do you think that is?
- ☐ How are children raised in your culture?
- ☐ What do you treasure from your grandparents?
- ☐ What values do you want to pass down to your children and family members one or two generations in the future?
- ☐ Do you remember any special celebration or family gathering? Explain in details.

140
Personal and Cultural
Report Checklist

U.S. President Report

Grades 3–6

The U.S. President report gives students a chance to research a president of their choice. This is an excellent opportunity to study one of our great leaders and their impact not only on our nation but the world. Students can use the president profile and time line to gather and organize their information. In addition, students should use index cards to take more detailed notes for each section of the profile and time line. Note that the profile and time line serve as a general overview to organize the report.

Students should choose a president of interest, unless they are drawing from a chosen class selection. They need to select several resources (books, newspaper articles, magazine articles, biographies, picture books) from the past and present about their president. Resources can include library reference materials, videos, or DVDs, and the Internet (e.g., whitehouse.gov, askforkids.com, or Google). Using the profile and time line as guides, students will take notes on index cards about key details of their president's life, including important dates, critical personal events, people who influenced him, major world events during his presidency, and so on. Once the notes (index cards) are gathered and students have the profiles and time lines completed, they are ready to draft their reports.

Reports start with a paragraph introducing the president and a brief history of his childhood. One to three paragraphs should then describe the president's adolescent and early adult years, possibly including his college years, marriage, political aspirations, and campaigning. The next one to three paragraphs will describe major events and significant issues that took place during his presidency. Students should include what their presidents stood for and what they were known for during their presidencies. Next, one to three paragraphs will describe his post-presidency life. Finally, the closing paragraph should summarize what students learned and what they think their president's legacy is.

Report Outline

1. One paragraph: introduction/childhood overview
2. One to three paragraphs: early life (pre-presidency)
3. One to three paragraphs: presidency (events/issues)
4. One to three paragraphs: post-presidency
5. One paragraph: conclusion (summary of what student learned)

Presidential Topics

These should be included in the report:

- Date and place of birth
- Parents, family background, occupations, traditions
- Brothers, sisters, and other close family members
- Education
- Important people or event(s) that shaped this person's character
- Career prior to presidency
- Marriage, children
- What led this person to run for president
- Political party affiliation
- This president's vice-president
- Important events/acts that occurred during this presidency
- Where this president lived after presidency
- Activities he participated in after his presidency
- Date and cause of death

U.S. PRESIDENT PROFILE

Name: _____   Date: _____

Teacher: _____   Class: _____

Personal Information

President's name: _____

Term/years in office: _____

Political party: _____

State: _____

Date of birth: _____

Family: _____

Interests/hobbies: _____

Illustration

Professional Information

Education: _____

Influences (events/people): _____

Pre-presidential career: _____

Inspiration for presidency: _____

Vice President: _____

Achievements: _____

_____

_____

Retirement: _____

Death: _____

U.S. PRESIDENT TIME LINE

EARLY LIFE

EVENT	DATE	NOTES
_____	_____	_____
_____	_____	_____
_____	_____	_____
_____	_____	_____
_____	_____	_____

PRESIDENCY

EVENT	DATE	NOTES
_____	_____	_____
_____	_____	_____
_____	_____	_____
_____	_____	_____
_____	_____	_____

POST-PRESIDENCY

EVENT	DATE	NOTES
_____	_____	_____
_____	_____	_____
_____	_____	_____
_____	_____	_____
_____	_____	_____

National Symbol Inventory
Grades K–6

A national symbol inventory report gives students the opportunity to explore icons of the United States that have significant importance and relevance to our nation and what it stands for. Using the national symbol inventory template as a research tool, students will begin their report by briefly discussing the symbol's background, history, and origin. They then will write about its national significance and what it represents to our country. Lastly, students will write about what it means to them. Students can include images or drawings of their symbol. The report should be three to four paragraphs in length.

Report Outline
1. One paragraph: background/history/origin
2. One to two paragraphs: significance/representation
3. One paragraph: personal significance

Significance
- What message does it give?
- Why does it represent what it stands for?
- Why do we need it?

What does it represent to the country?
- What message does it give about our country?
- What American value does it promote/stand for?

What does it mean to you?
- What does it mean to you personally?
- Why did you choose it?
- Have you seen it? What was that experience like?
- What value or tradition does it symbolize in your life?
- Sketch a picture of the symbol.

Name: _____ Date: _____ Class: _____

NATIONAL SYMBOL INVENTORY

Name of symbol: _____

Year built/established: _____ Built/established by: _____

Significance
_____
_____
_____

What does it represent to the country?
_____
_____
_____

What does it mean to you?
_____
_____
_____

Sketch a picture of the symbol.

143
National Symbol Inventory

State Report

Grades 2–6

A state report gives students a chance to research a state and learn about the diversity of our nation. Students should choose a state of interest or select one from a list of designated states. Students can select several resources such as books, newspaper/magazine articles, or picture books about their state of choice. To find resources, they can use the Internet (ask.com, Google), the library, or videos/DVDs.

Students should consider important dates in the history of their state, critical events that take/took place in their state, and people who inhabit their state. Notes should include key information on the state, such as the capital, current population, climate, geography, industries, agricultural products, and state symbols. The state profile can serve as a guide and help students organize information.

The report should start with a paragraph introducing the state and the main ideas to be covered. The next paragraph describes the state's geography and gives information on its location, major bodies of water, highest and lowest points, and landforms. Students can even include a map of the state. The next paragraph should discuss the climate of the state, including whether it is hot, mild, or cold and whether it experiences any extreme weather patterns. Examples should be given of conditions at different times of the year. The next paragraph should give the latest population figure, how its size ranks in terms of other states, and what residents do for a living. The state's major industries and agricultural products should be identified. Next is a paragraph that discusses state symbols. In this paragraph, students should write about and illustrate the state flag, including when it was adopted. Then they can discuss any symbols applicable to their state: state bird, state insect, state reptile, state fossil, state dinosaur, state rock, state song, and state dance. To end their report, students will share what is special or unique about their state. Students may list national parks, national monuments, historic battlefields, important places, or historic events that happened in their state. This paragraph can serve as their conclusion.

Students can use the illustration page to create a postcard for their state and illustrate state symbols.

State Topics

These should be included in the report:

- Date of statehood
- State capital
- State flower
- State bird
- State tree
- State fish
- State flag
- State seal
- State population
- State geography
- Bordering states
- State climate
- State resources
- State agriculture
- State industry
- State monuments
- State parks
- State historical events

Report Outline

1. One paragraph: state introduction/topics to be discussed
2. One paragraph: state geography
3. One paragraph: state climate
4. One paragraph: state population/industry
5. One paragraph: state symbols
6. One paragraph: state's uniqueness/conclusion

Name: ______________________ Date: ______________ Class: ______________

STATE PROFILE 1

State Name: ______________________

State Flower: ______________________

Date of Statehood: ______________________

State Bird: ______________________

State Capital: ______________________

State Tree: ______________________

State Population: ______________________

State Fish: ______________________

State Flag:

State Seal:

State Geography/Location: ______________________

____

Bordering States: ______________________

State Climate: ______________________

State Resources: ______________________

State Agriculture: ______________________

State Industry: ______________________

State Monuments: ______________________

State Parks: ______________________

State Historical Events: ______________________

____

____

____

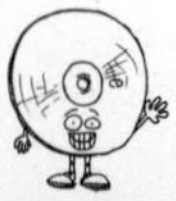

State Bird

State Tree

State Industry

State Flag

State Flower

State Resources

State Agricultural Products

Name: _____

Date: _____

Teacher: _____

Class: _____

Welcome to . . .

Draw your state here.

Color and label the states. Star and label the capitals.

Community Exploration Group Activity
Grades K–2

Prior to this activity, discuss what makes up a neighborhood and label a smaller scale model of one, pointing out the background and foreground. Then on several sections of large white butcher paper, draw the background and foreground for a neighborhood and have students paint them with tempera paints. You may want to use three to four sheets so that the students have enough areas to paint.

Once the students have finished painting the background and foreground of the neighborhood and the pieces are dry, tape the pieces together. Have students draw and color all the components that make up their neighborhood, including schools, post office, grocery stores, parks, empty lots, skyscrapers, and so on. Attach pictures to the painted butcher paper to signify the locations of such places. Also, have students make (or use the templates provided in the following pages) construction paper homes and apartment buildings and label them with their names so that they can glue them onto the neighborhood.

Materials

scissors
crayons
tempera paints
butcher paper
construction paper
glue or glue sticks

 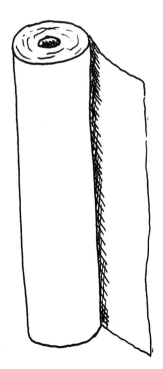 

COMMUNITY VOCABULARY

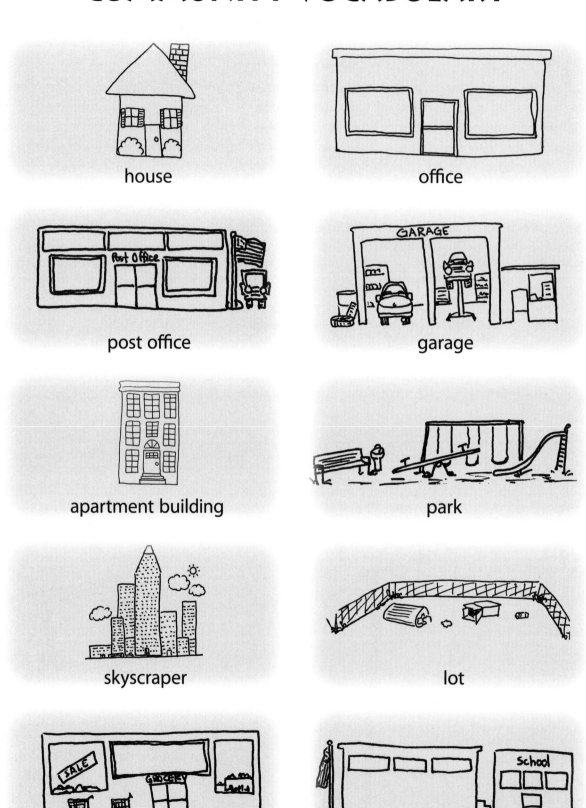

house

office

post office

garage

apartment building

park

skyscraper

lot

store

school

HOUSE TEMPLATE

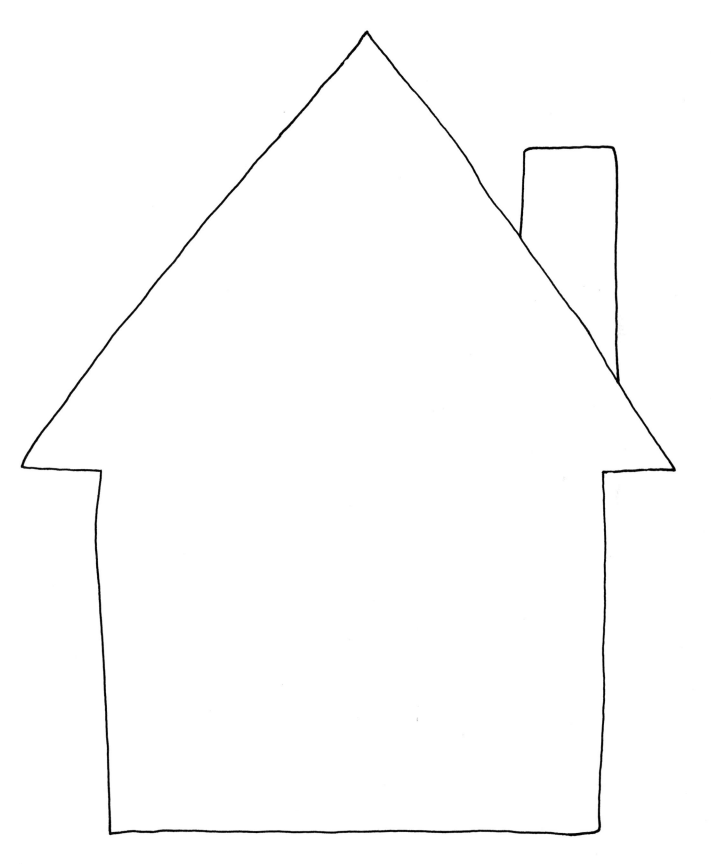

APARTMENT BUILDING TEMPLATE

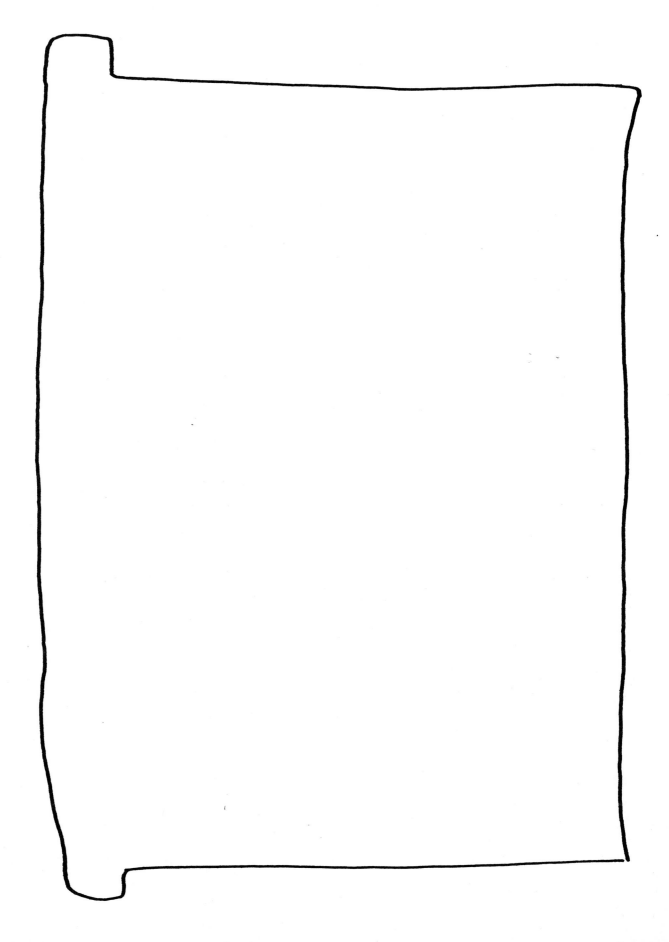

BUILDING TEMPLATE

Name: _____

Date: _____

Draw your community.

Label the community buildings. **Word Bank:** building   house   apartments

_____   _____   _____

Careers in Your Community
Grades K–2

Careers are a big part of primary education and an important part of a student's understanding of community. Students love to explore and learn about the many jobs in their community. This report deals with a few of those jobs that students should be familiar with. Add in any additional jobs that relate to your specific community.

Here is our list of community helpers:

Police Officer	Nurse	Doctor
Lawyer	Teacher	Crossing Guard
Firefighter	Mom/Dad	Sanitation Worker
Transportation Provider	Lifeguard	Store Clerk

Students will select the career of their choice to investigate. They will conduct an interview of 5 to 10 questions with someone in that career. With the support of a parent or guardian, they will need to make an appointment with the person to be interviewed. They will interview the person and record their responses, again supported by an adult. The answers will be recorded as complete sentences or in a simple paragraph, depending on the grade. Students will finish their report telling whether or not they would like to have this job. If possible, students can take pictures of their community helper and where he or she works. Students then will illustrate their community helper using the template provided, or they can simply illustrate their helper as they see them at work.

Possible Interview Questions

- What does he or she do? What is his or her career?
- Why is his or her job important to the community?
- How does he or she do this job?
- What training is necessary to do the job?
- How long has he or she been doing this job?
- What are the best parts of the job?
- What are the worst parts of the job?

COMMUNITY HELPER VOCABULARY

Crossing Guard

Doctor

Transportation Provider

Firefighter

Attorney

Lifeguard

Stay-at-Home Mom or Dad

Nurse

Police Officer

Teacher

Sanitation Worker

Store Clerk

152
Community Helper Vocabulary

Name: _____

Community Helper: _____

Location: _____ Date: _____

COMMUNITY HELPER INTERVIEW

What do you do?
_____
_____
_____

What is your occupation?
_____
_____
_____

What skills or equipment do you use for your job?
_____
_____
_____

What people do you help in your job?
_____
_____
_____

How did you learn to do your job?
_____
_____
_____

How long have you been doing this job?
_____
_____
_____

What parts of your job do you like the most?
_____
_____
_____

What parts of your job do you like the least?
_____
_____
_____

Thank you!

Name:

Date:

COMMUNITY HELPER TEMPLATE

All About Me Report
Grades K–2

Primary students focus on their place in the world. It is important that they understand who they are and their uniqueness. They are starting to understand that everyone is different and together we all have a part in our community. This recognition begins with the self. An All About Me report lets students learn about themselves and gives them a chance to share their uniqueness with others.

An All About Me profile helps pull together personal information to complete the report and information teachers can use to get to know their students. Parents can assist younger students in completing this profile. Once the profile is returned to school, students can use this information to write their reports. Teachers can highlight sections that are being used or even cut the sentences into strips and have students order them and then glue them down on a separate piece of paper. Students can then copy their sentences to create a report. Advanced students can work independently by using the All About Me web and profile to assist them in their writing. The web can be completed to model the pre-writing phase of the writing process. As the teacher, you can choose the best method of creating this report. Students can create self-portraits to go with their reports.

Create an All About Me silhouette by tracing a student's silhouette onto a large piece of butcher paper. Create word banks in and around the silhouette with words that tell about "Me." This can be left up all year for students to refer to.

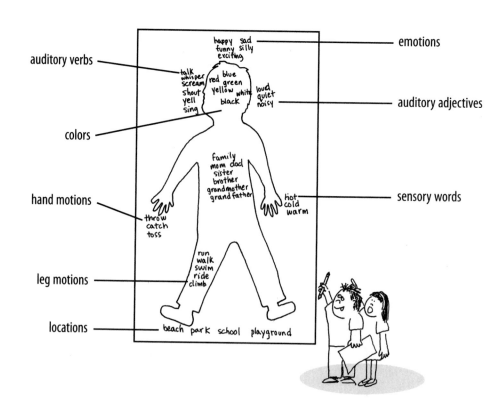

- Be creative
- Personalize
- Refer to silhouette
- Add to silhouette

All About Me Profile 1

My name is _____

My address is _____

My phone number is _____

My favorite food is _____

My favorite color is _____

My favorite game is _____

My favorite TV show is _____

My favorite subject in school is _____

I have _____

My friends are _____

My pet is _____

All About Me Profile 2

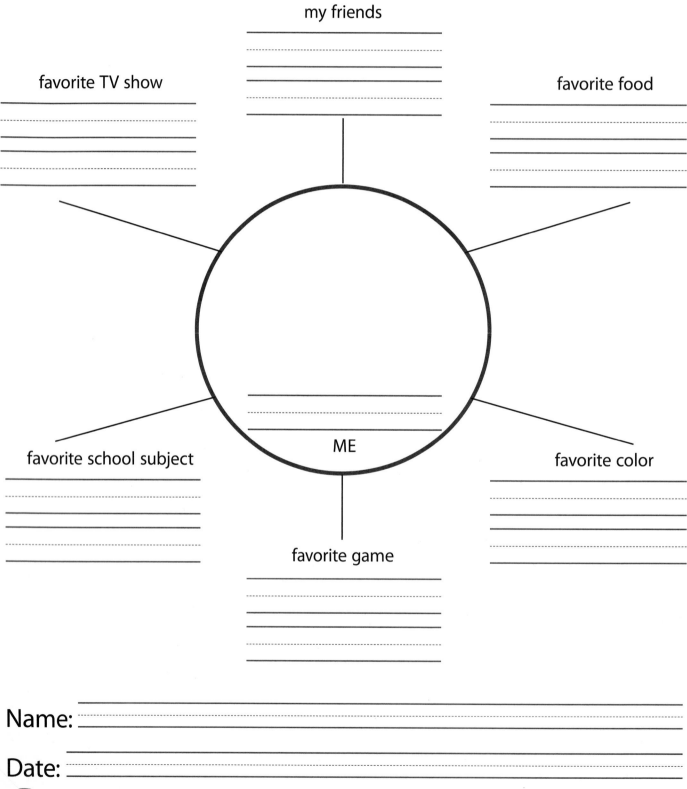

my friends

favorite TV show

favorite food

favorite school subject

ME

favorite color

favorite game

Name:

Date:

My friends are

_____
_____
_____
_____

All About Me Book

My name is

_____

I am _____ years old.

My favorite color is

_____

My favorite food is

_____

My favorite TV show is _____

My favorite game is _____

My favorite school activity is _____

Country Report
Grades 2–6

The Country Report is an exciting way to learn about world geography and different cultures. Today more than ever our world is becoming a smaller place thanks to technology such as the Internet. Students can use these reports as a chance to learn and share what they discover about their selected country.

Students can select from a chosen pool of countries or a country they are interested in, depending on your instructional goals. Students need to select several resources such as books, newspaper articles, magazine articles, and picture books from the past and present to locate information about their countries. Try the Internet (ask.com, Google), the library, or videos/DVDs. Students need to take notes on key facts about their countries, such as important dates, critical events that took place (or are happening now) in the country, and the people who live there. As part of their reports, students should note key facts, such as the capital, current population figures, climate, geography (mountains, lakes, rivers, deserts), industries, agricultural products, and country symbols. The country profile provided can serve as a guide and overview. Notes can be taken on index cards for easy organization.

The introductory paragraph will state the main ideas the report will focus on. Next, the student needs a paragraph that gives information on the country's location in relation to the United States and describes the country's geography, including major bodies of water, highest and lowest points, and landforms. A country map should be included. The next paragraph addresses the country's climate. Is it hot, mild, or cold? Is there an extreme climate or weather pattern? Examples of the weather at different times of the year should be included. The students then add a paragraph about the country's population, including the latest data. How does it rank with other countries? What do citizens do for a living? What are the major industries and agricultural products? The following paragraph describes symbols of the country, including what the country flag looks like and when it was adopted. Students can draw a picture of the flag. Some countries have special symbols, such as a national bird, song, or dance that can be included. The final paragraph should describe what is special about the country—what it has that other countries do not have. Students should describe the food, traditions, clothing, and spoken languages. This paragraph can serve as their conclusion.

Country Topics

These should be included in the report:

- Country geography
- Geographic location
- Country map
- Climate
- Weather
- Population
- Economics
- Agriculture
- Industry
- Flag
- Symbols
- Food
- Traditions
- Clothing
- Languages

Report Outline

1. One paragraph: country introduction/topics to be discussed
2. One paragraph: country geography
3. One paragraph: country climate
4. One paragraph: country population/industry
5. One paragraph: country symbols
6. One paragraph: country uniqueness/conclusion

COUNTRY PROFILE

Country Name: _____

National Capital: _____

State Capital: _____

Population: _____

National Flower: _____

National Bird: _____

National Symbols: _____

Year Established: _____

National Flag:

National Seal:

Geography/Location: _____

_____

Bordering Countries: _____

Climate: _____

Resources: _____

Agriculture: _____

Industry: _____

Languages: _____

Tourism: _____

Historical Events: _____

_____

_____

_____

Name: _____ Date: _____

Draw your country and label significant elements such as the capital, major cities, land formations, and bodies of water.

Key

N W E S

National Flag Report
Grades 2–6

One of the most powerful symbols of any nation is its flag. Each flag is unique to its own country and has its own history. As students learn about their country, studying their nation's flag has important significance. As they move beyond their country and study other nations, flags can provide them with a rich history. From the colors and symbols to their placement on a flag, each country has designed its flag to represent who they are as a nation and people. Knowing the history of one's flag fosters patriotism. Knowing the history of another nation's flag in turn fosters respect. Use the following template as a guide for creating a National Flag Report.

History

When was the flag adopted? What was happening during this time?
Were there previous versions? Why did it change?
Who designed the flag? Who proposed the flag?

Significance

What do the colors represent? What does their placement represent?
What do the symbols or images on the flag represent?

Protocol

How is the flag displayed? When is it displayed? Are there special occasions in which the flag is displayed?
Is there a protocol for hanging the flag? Is there a protocol for protecting the flag? Storing the flag?
Are there special protocols (for example, distress signal, a national tragedy, and so forth)?
Is there any reason why a flag must be destroyed? What is considered disrespectful toward the flag?
Are there any laws involving the flag?

Traditions

Are there any songs or poems about the flag?
Where can the flag most commonly be found?
Are there any traditions involving the flag (for example, giving it to the widow of a fallen soldier)?

Flag Report

1. Select a country's flag and complete organizer.
2. Write a brief introduction about your country and its flag.
3. For each of the organizer's areas, create a paragraph about those aspects of the flag.
4. Conclude your report with a summary of what the flag represents to you.
5. Create the flag for the country you have chosen.

NATIONAL FLAG REPORT

COUNTRY BACKGROUND

Country Name: _____

Location: _____

Population: _____

Government: _____

FLAG HISTORY

Adoption Date: _____

Overview: What was happening during this time?

FLAG

Designed the flag: _____ Proposed the flag: _____

Time Line: Illustrate earlier designs and write the date underneath. If there are no earlier versions, use boxes for flag elements and labels.

FLAG SIGNIFICANCE

Colors: Explain what the colors and their placement represent.

Symbol/Image: Explain what the symbol/s and/or image/s represent.

NATIONAL FLAG REPORT

PROTOCOL

Displaying the flag: How and when is the flag displayed, hung, and stored? Are there any exceptions?

Protecting the flag: How is the flag protected? Are there laws to protect the flag? Is it ever destroyed?

TRADITIONS

Songs/Poems: Are there songs or poems that have been written about the flag?

Traditions: Is the flag traditionally displayed for certain holidays? Is the flag ever given out as part of a ceremony?

IN YOUR OWN WORDS

What does the flag mean to you? What does it represent? If it is not your country's flag, describe what it would mean to a national of that country.

NATIONAL FLAG

Name: _____ Date: _____

Illustrate the national flag of the country you have selected. Write the name of the country and your name on the back. The flag can be cut out and displayed or attached to your flag report.

Art

This chapter will include samples of "wow 'em" art-project ideas and techniques that can be used as culminating projects for curricular area themes. These projects can help motivate students and get them excited about learning. It includes the how-tos, strategies, and recipes needed for making successful projects. Included are ideas for crayon-resist, collage, and papier-mâché projects.

Papier-Mâché

Papier-mâché is an easy and inexpensive way to create sculptures from torn paper and homemade paste. It is a motivating project that can support learning across the curriculum. Papier-mâché sculptures can serve as culminating projects for science and social science themes and for holiday celebrations. Sculptures can even be used to create characters from literature units. Because papier-mâché uses recycled materials to create the sculptures, it naturally leads to teaching the value of recycling.

Papier-mâché involves pasting strips of paper over molds (balloons, taped newspaper shapes, paper towel tubes) using a simple flour, water, and salt-based paste. These forms are assembled into animals, figures, or just about any shape. Once dry, the sculptures can be painted and decorated.

The following is an overview of materials, steps, and tips for making papier-mâché. There are several variations, and it is important for you to try different strategies to see what works best for you. Have fun. The only way to learn what works best for you is to do it!

Materials

measuring spoon
flour
water
salt
mixing bowl
measuring cup
plastic tablecloth/
   plastic garbage bag
masking tape
newspaper
molds
smock
glue
starch

Papier-Mâché Paste

flour
't
ps water

Alternative Papier-Mâché Pastes

½ cup white glue OR liquid starch
½ cup of water

Steps

1. *Prepare the area:* Papier-mâché can get messy, so cover the work space/table. A plastic garbage bag, which can be opened at the seam, or a plastic tablecloth can be taped to the table. (Plastic keeps the projects from sticking to the table.)

2. *Prepare the paper:* Tear newspaper or newsprint into strips about 1–1½ inches wide by 4 inches long. Tearing the paper with the grain of the paper gives a straight-line tear. You can test the paper by tearing it, and you will know when you are tearing with the grain because it tears straight. The number of strips needed depends on the size of the project. You can always tear more.

3. *Prepare the paste:* Start with a large mixing bowl. For easier cleanup, it helps to line it first with doubled plastic shopping bags. Some teachers make the mixture on a stove to get a smooth consistency. Warm water can also be used. Start with a cup of water and the flour. Once this is mixed, slowly add and mix in the rest of the water. Mix the mixture with your hands as it is easier to break up the lumps. Continue to mix the ingredients to the consistency of a heavy whipping cream, not like yogurt. There are alternative recipes using glue or starch. With all recipes it is a good idea to test them and see what works best before performing this activity with your students.

Paste
1 cup flour
1½–2 cups water
2 T salt

4. *Dip the paper:* Place/lay one strip of newspaper at a time into the paste so the strip is completely covered. Lift the strip out of the paste. Hold the strip above the paste and remove excess paste by running it through the index and middle fingers of your other hand.

5. ***Place the strips:*** Wrap the strips over the mold, balloon, or form one at a time. Once completely covered, allow the form to dry. Apply consecutive strip layers until desired hardness is achieved. Most projects need three to four layers unless weight is an issue, in which case two layers should work. More than three layers can be used to create a sturdier, stronger object.

    Note: Using different color newsprint can be helpful in the layering process. You can see when new layers are complete. Blank newsprint (even a brown paper bag) can be used as a last layer to cover up the newspaper layers and keep them from showing through.

6. ***Build project:*** Some projects need several parts adhered to the form. For example, an animal needs legs and a head. The body can be assembled using simple, lightweight forms and masking tape. Simple lightweight forms include plastic bottles, paper tubes, balloons, cereal boxes, and plastic bags filled with newspaper balls. Even newspaper can be fashioned into parts with masking tape to create mass and form. These can be glued on or taped on with masking tape. This is an excellent opportunity to discuss recycling! You can also use a mold. It is a good idea to grease molds with petroleum jelly first for easy removal.

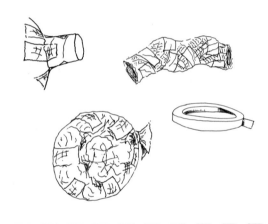

7. ***Paint project:*** Projects need to air dry one to two days prior to painting. Rotating the project will help it dry evenly. Projects must be completely dry prior to painting. If it is cool to the touch, then it needs more time to dry. It is important to let projects dry in a well-ventilated area as molding can occur if drying is too slow. Salt in the paste helps prevent molding. Once dry, projects can be lightly sanded to smooth their surfaces. Priming the project white can help cover newspaper print but is not necessary. Acrylic paints and poster paints can be used to paint projects. Tempera paint can also be used and may be more readily available. However, tempera is not as shiny as acrylic or poster paints. Painting finished projects helps to prevent molding, and pieces of colored tissue paper can be added to the wet paint for a nice effect.

    Note: Projects can be varnished with a layer of white glue watered down slightly with water. Try it first on a test project and est the best mixture of water to glue.

lay and share: Share, dialogue, and write about projects!

Creative Collages

Collages can be done in several ways using a variety of materials. Students can cut paper into shapes and glue them in a manner that creates a scene or image. A theme-based poster collage can be composed of cut out images or words. Regardless of how you decide to create your collage, it can be used across the curriculum to creatively incorporate art. Collages allow students to be creative and demonstrate an understanding of the content.

Materials

tempera paint
magazines
scissors
pen and pencil
paper
brushes
glue

Steps

1. *Prepare collage paper:* Using several colors of paint, have students cover a heavy quality of paper with whatever color they want to set off their collage.

2. *Cut shapes:* After the paint dries, have students cut out different shapes to be used in designing images related to whatever they are studying. For example, shapes to create desert animals if studying an arid habitat or circles of various sizes to create planets, stars, moon, and so forth if learning about the solar system. Students can also lightly sketch out their pieces related to the theme or simply use random shapes.

3. **Assemble shapes:** Have students arrange their shapes to create the image they desire. They can then glue the shapes into place.

4. **Share/Display:** Let the collages dry completely. Then the students can share their work with the class or display it on a bulletin board. Students can also write stories or explanations about their collages.

Hint

Instead of using painted paper, you can use the following:

- Decorative paper (wrapping paper, scrapbooking paper)
- Line patterns
- Newspaper
- Wallpaper samples
- Calendar pictures

Setups/Uses

Collages can be used across the curriculum. They can be abstract or theme-based.

Dioramas

Dioramas can be used across the curriculum, and they are great for bringing thematic units to life. By having students explain what they have created, these dioramas can be a meaningful way for second-language learners to express and develop their oral language skills.

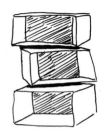

Materials

tape
scissors
string
crayons
glue
markers
paper
various boxes

Steps

1. **Prepare box:** Cut the box so that one end is open. Depending on what types of boxes you use, this may or may not be an easy process. You want to have one side open and the other sides closed. Shoe boxes are simple to use as they already have an open side.

2. **Cover box:** Although covering the box with paper isn't necessary, if you want to do so, do it now. Choose a paper to cover the entire box and glue it down. Wrapping paper that matches the theme of the diorama is quick and easy. Construction paper and butcher paper are also good choices.

3. **Select theme:** If the whole class isn't working on a common theme, have students decide what theme they want in their dioramas and then have them sketch their ideas on paper.

4. ***Create background:*** Lay the back of the box on desired background and trace. Cut out paper, which now fits the back of the box. Draw a picture on the background paper and color. When finished, glue the background to the inside bottom of the box.

5. ***Create items for scene:*** Cut out, design, and color items that will go inside the diorama. *Always leave extra paper at the base for standing up the items to be glued in the box.* Inexpensive plastic figurines, bought from a store, can also be used.

6. ***Stand and arrange components:*** Fold the flaps on the items designed for the diorama. Arrange items so they all face forward and are visible.

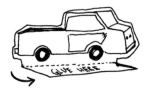

7. ***Glue:*** Glue diorama pieces inside the box. Glue items one at a time, keeping arrangement intact.

8. ***Write and share:*** When dioramas are complete, students can write about them and share them with each other and the class.

Hint

You can use the string to hang items in your diorama.

Mobiles

Mobile making is a multistep project that can be accomplished over several days. The finished product is wonderful and fascinating to students. Included here are directions on how to make a simple mobile as well as variations depending on your available materials. Remember, mobiles come in many different shapes and sizes.

| coat hanger | wire | chopstick/skewer | sentence strip | straws |

Materials

various papers
straws
popsicle sticks
coat hangers
string
tape
crayons
scissors
needles
thread
markers
other items

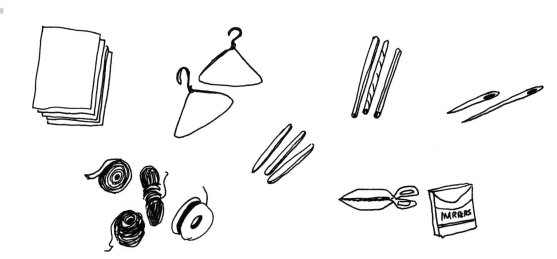

Steps

1. *Plan mobile:* Plan what the theme of the mobile will be. Sketch out ideas and the items to be hung from the mobile.

279

2. ***Draw and color:*** Draw mobile items. Keep size in mind so all items will fit and can be seen. Color and decorate items using markers and crayons. Various types of paper can be used to make mobiles more interesting. Plain index cards (3 × 5 or 5 × 7) are perfect choices for paper as they are sturdy and keep sizes to a minimum.

3. ***Cut out items:*** Cut out items so they are ready to go on the mobile. Again, keep size in mind, so all can fit, be seen, and hang free.

4. ***Assemble mobile frame:*** Using straws, popsicle sticks, coat hangers, chopsticks, skewers, or wire, put together the mobile frame from which to hang items.

5. ***Attach string/yarn:*** From the frame of the mobile, tie strings that cutout pieces will hang from. Vary the lengths of the strings to create an interesting mobile.

6. ***Attach items:*** Attach items to the free end of the string. A hole punch can be used to make the hole. Do not make the hole too close to the edge, as it might tear. You can also hang pieces by using a needle to thread string through the paper. This creates a smaller hole and is less likely to tear. Use a small piece of tape at the hole for reinforcement.

7. ***Attach hanging string/yarn:*** Attach string/yarn at the center top of mobile to hang it. Students can share and explain their mobiles. Being able to talk about their work is an important part of making art!

Paper Mosaic

Similar to a collage, a mosaic involves gluing small pieces of paper onto a larger sheet. A mosaic, however, yields to a specific image or design, which is made up of many small pieces. Mosaics are commonly seen all around us, usually in tile on tabletops or on walls to create amazing images. Students can create their own mosaics with small bits and pieces of construction paper. It just takes some creativity, planning, and time. Mosaics are a great way to incorporate creativity and art across the curriculum. Mosaics can be portraits, landscapes, wildlife, architecture, or anything that can be linked to a particular area of study.

Materials

colored paper (construction, art paper, and so forth)
glue
pencil
scissors

Steps

1. Sketch out the subject of the piece. This should be just a line drawing with no shading or extreme detail.

2. Cut selected paper into small pieces. These can be a variety of irregular shapes or regular shapes, such as small squares or triangles. Their size would depend on the amount of detail you want in the piece and time available to complete the mosaic.

3. Select an area on your picture to begin, and start gluing in the pieces. It can be helpful to lay a few down and play with placement prior to gluing, just to get a feel for how the pieces will come together. Apply only a small amount of glue to the back of the piece and then place it on the page. Continue, placing each piece down next to another staying in the lines of your sketch.

4. While working on the mosaic, step back from it now and then to see how it is coming together. Up close it may not look like your sketch, but as you step back you will begin to see your picture.

Tips

- A good rule of thumb is that the younger the student, the larger the pieces should be.

- Use slightly darker shades to create shadows and demonstrate changes in values.

- Place same-color shapes in food storage bags or small containers with lids as a way to organize them until you are ready to work.

- Pieces can be torn instead of cut for a different look and texture.

- Pieces can be glued close together or even overlapping for different effects.

- Consider the size; mosaics can take a great deal of time. If you are too ambitious, students may not finish their mosaics.

- Try tracing a shamrock or heart, cut it into shapes, and then glue them to another sheet of paper (close but not touching) as a mosaic.

- Words and letters can also be done in mosaics.

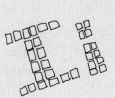

Tissue Paper Art

Tissue paper is commonly available to most classroom teachers. It comes in a variety of colors and can be used to create beautiful pictures, portraits, and other images related the subjects studied. Tissue paper art is another excellent way to infuse the arts across the curriculum, giving students an opportunity to creatively demonstrate what they have learned. Because tissue paper art requires careful hands, it works best with older students, but it can be done at lower grades with support. You will need only a few items to get started.

Materials

tissue paper
glue or liquid starch
paint brush
heavy drawing paper
scissors
pencil
Sharpie (optional)

Steps

1. Thin out the glue with a little water so that it is easier to brush on, or use a liquid starch. Set aside in a small bowl for use when ready.

2. Sketch out your picture. Use only simple lines, with no shading.

3. Cut out shapes of tissue paper that approximately match the shapes in your drawing.

4. Using your brush, apply a small amount of glue or liquid starch to the area you have selected to glue your tissue paper cutout.

5. Place cutout on drawing, onto the paper where you applied the small amount of glue or liquid starch.

6. Gently apply more glue or liquid starch over the entire piece of tissue paper. BE CAREFUL not to move or tear the tissue paper.

7. Continue adding pieces of tissue paper until picture is complete. Always consider whether you need more or less glue or liquid starch. You want the paper to be covered, but not dripping.

8. Allow the picture to dry. Use a Sharpie, if permissible, or a black felt tip marker to outline images and add detail.

Tips

- As a variation, dark silhouettes of objects, people, or buildings can be drawn in. This adds more detail and gives foreground to the piece.

- As the paper dries, it may need to be flattened out. Once it is no longer sticky, place the tissue paper art between a few books and leave it overnight.

Ir-resist-ible Art!

Resist art is very easy and very simple to do. The resist part of this project can be done using crayons or glue. Both achieve the same outcome, but they give different looks. Students love to make this project!

Materials

glue
flour and water
crayons
watercolor paints
oil pastels
various papers

Steps

1. *Sketch:* Have students lightly sketch out their drawings on a piece of paper. Try using different color papers for this. Black paper looks great using glue and oil pastels!

2. *Trace:* After completing the initial sketch, students trace over the lines using glue, crayons, or oil pastels. All three will resist a paint wash. Instead of glue you can use a paste mixture of one-third flour and two-thirds water (this is more involved, so try it on your own first). Each method gives a different effect.

285

3. **Color:** After the glue line dries, use the oil pastels or crayons to color the picture. Or if using only crayon/oil pastels (no glue), just use those to color the page. Make sure outlines are dark to assure the resist effect. The overall coloring job does not need to fill every part of the paper as resist wash will cover the page.

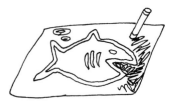

4. **Wash:** Using watercolor paint (experiment with different dilutions and see what works best for your project), wash over picture (entirely or only the part that you want to resist). For a different but equally beautiful look, try using watercolors to color in the picture over the glue.

5. **Dry, share, and discuss:** Allow to dry. Have students share and discuss their work. Encourage your students to talk about their pieces. Explaining artwork is powerful for oral language development.

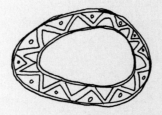

Hint

Resist art can be done when making picture frames. It will make pictures POP!

Scratch Art

Scratch art is an activity that requires scratching away a surface of black paint to reveal the white or bright colors underneath. This art can be done using a premade board from the store where all you need to do is scratch away your picture. But scratchboard can be expensive and very delicate for students to work with. The inexpensive alternative is to make your own scratchboard, which is durable and easy for students to make. Scratch art can be used to add to other art pieces, or it can make great book covers. Just follow these directions!

Materials

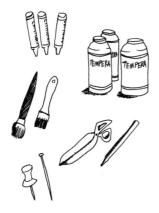

crayons
black tempera paint
thick paintbrushes
thumbtack
pencil
needle
scissors

Steps

1. **Color:** Using several different color crayons, cover the entire piece of paper.

2. **Paint:** Paint over the crayon-colored side of the paper with black tempera paint. Let the paint dry completely.

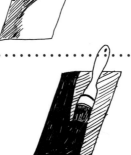

3. **Scratch:** After the paint is dry, use scissors or a sewing needle to scratch out a picture. Be careful to scratch only through the black paint and not through the paper.

4. **Display:** The colorful crayon shows through and your picture is complete!

Silhouettes

Silhouettes are easy to do and require very little prep time, but they provide strong images. All you need is sunshine!

Materials

pencil
black marker
paper
eraser
black tempera paint
flashlight, lamp, or sun
thick paintbrush

Steps

1. *Mount paper:* Start by taping the paper to the wall where the shadow will be cast. If you're in the sun, chances are you will be placing the paper on the ground.

2. **Position student:** Have the student stand in front of the paper so his or her shadow will be cast on the paper.

3. *Cast shadow:* You can use the sun or an alternate source of light to cast the shadow. Different sources, such as a flashlight or overhead projector, can cast a shadow. Use whatever is easy and convenient!

4. *Trace shadow:* Have students work together. While one student holds the light, another student casts the shadow, and a third student traces the shadow. Younger ages may require more help from the teacher.

5. *Retrace and fill:* After the shadow is traced with pencil, trace it again using a black marker. When you have finished tracing it with the marker, have the students use black tempera paint to fill in the silhouette.

6. *Dry:* Hang until all the paint is dry, or place them flat on a table if you don't want paint to run.

Hints

- Try making silhouettes of different body parts and different objects. This project can expand as far as you would like it to go!
- Try using a black paper. Trace in pencil or white chalk, and then cut out the silhouette and mount onto another paper.
- Use the silhouette as a background. Mount a writing paper or an illustration page inside of the silhouette to write or draw about the silhouette.
- Have students create other silhouettes by cutting images from black construction paper and make a collage (e.g., dinosaurs, their own shadow, and so on).

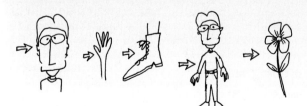

Mat Weaving

Weaving is an indigenous art form practiced all over the world. Fun and easy to do, mat weaving looks great. This project can be done for many holidays or just for fun.

Materials

paper bags
scissors
tape
paper

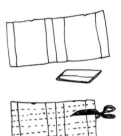

Steps

1. *Prepare bag:* Take a paper bag and cut it down the seam, removing the bottom of the bag. One large flat piece will be needed.

2. *Cut strips:* Cut the large piece of paper bag into 2-inch strips. You're going to need several strips to complete the mat.

3. *Prepare strips:* Gently crumple strips to soften them. Be careful not to tear them when preparing their softness.

4. *Mount to desk:* Tape the strips to the side of the desk where the students can begin to do their weaving. Tape them to the middle of the desk for younger students.

5. *Weave:* After the strips are taped to the desk, start by weaving in one strip at a time—under, over, under, over. Then alternate the pattern—over, under, over, under. Continue to add strips until the desired length is reached.

6. *Tie off:* Once all the strips are in and the mat is complete, untape the mat from the desk. The ends of the strips can be folded over and woven in or trimmed off, and the sides can be taped.

▶ Hints ◀

- Try different-colored paper for the alternate strips, or choose from a variety of materials, such as yarn, strips of felt, ribbon, and so on. Also, the mats can be covered with contact paper making them waterproof. They make great cultural
ble mats!

can create a portable cardboard loom that can be easily stored. Make a series
s at both ends of the cardboard. Weave one continuous string from slit to slit
d the board.

Kid Clay

Students, especially younger ones, love to play with play dough. Making clay in the classroom is easy and an excellent way to motivate your students. Kid clay can be used to make almost anything, from necklaces and ornaments to model figures studied in social studies. The possibilities are endless. As with any art project, it is a good idea to try this activity prior to using it with your class. Enjoy!

Materials

bowl
flour
cup
pan
food coloring
salt
straw
spoon
tempera paint
water
yarn
wax paper

Recipe

3–4 cups flour
1 cup salt
1 T vegetable oil
(optional, but makes it easier to knead)

Steps

1. *Mix flour and salt:* Mix dry ingredients together in large mixing bowl.

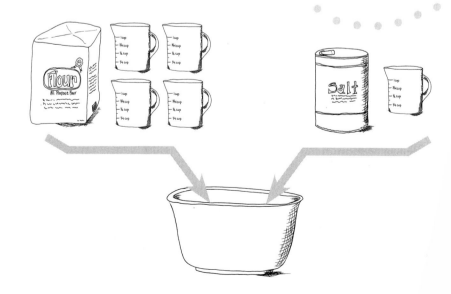

2. *Add water:* Slowly add water to the dry mixture, mixing ingredients together. Add food coloring or tempera paint for color (optional). Water can be warmed in a separate pan for better mixing.

3. *Mix ingredients:* Knead until mixed well. If mixture is too dry (crumbly), add water; if it is too wet (sticky), add flour. Wax paper can make a good work surface.

4. *Create your sculpture:* Create beads or figures. Don't make them too large as drying becomes difficult. Make beads, if desired, using a straw. Push a hole through bead.

5. *Dry sculpture:* Air dry for up to one week. Baking is an option. Warm at 100°C in oven. Time depends on thickness, but do not exceed 200°C. *Be careful to not overbake.* If clay is browning but not done, cover with foil.

6. *Add the finishing touch:* Paint with tempera or acrylic. Varnish/glaze with a clear varnish (optional).

Note: It is best to use clay mixture within two days. The clay can be stored in an airtight container in a refrigerator, which can extend its life.

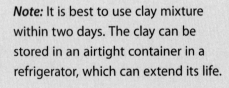

Suggested Resources

Children's Literature References

Adam, W. (2000). *Telling Time.* Dover Publications. ISBN 0486407942.

Adler, D. (1996). *Fraction Fun.* Holiday House, Inc. ISBN 0823412598.

Blakey, N. (1996). *Lotions, Potions, and Slime.* Ten Speed Press. ISBN 188367221X.

Branley, F. (1996). *What Makes a Magnet?* HarperCollins Children's Books. ISBN 0064451488.

Bredeson, C. (2003). *Lift Off!* Scholastic, Inc. ISBN 0516269542.

Butterfield, M. (2000). *Learning Clock.* Barnes and Noble Books. ISBN 0760719160.

Campbell-Ernst, L. (2005). *Tangram Magician.* Handprint Books. ISBN 1593541066.

Carle, E. (1994). *The Very Hungry Caterpillar.* Penguin Young Readers Group. ISBN 0399226901.

Carle, E. (1991). *The Tiny Seed.* Simon & Schuster Children's. ISBN 088708155X.

Carmi, R. (2002). *Amazing Magnetism.* Scholastic, Inc. ISBN 0439314321.

Cool, J. (2003). *Toast: 60 Ways to Butter Your Bread and Then Some.* Chronicle Books LLE. ISBN 081185553.

Crum, S. (2001). *Who Took My Hairy Toe?* Albert Whitman Publishers. ISBN 0807559725.

Daly, K. (2005). *The Good Humor Man.* Golden Books. ISBN 0375832807.

Dobson, C. (2003). *Pizza Counting Book.* Charlesbridge Publishing, Inc. ISBN 0881063398.

Dodds, D. (1996). *Shape of Things.* Candlewick Press. ISBN 1564026981.

Elder, V. (1997). *Flubber: My Story.* Disney Press. ISBN 0786842008.

Erlback, A. (1995). *Peanut Butter.* Lerner Publishing Group. ISBN 0822597098.

Fitzgibbon, K. (1999). *Geometry for Primary Grades.* Steck-Vaughn Publishers. ISBN 0817258078.

Flaherty, M. (2004). *Electricity and Batteries.* Stargazer Books. ISBN 1932799680.

Gardner, R. (2004). *Electricity and Magnetism: Science Fair Projects Using Batteries, Balloons, and Other Hair-Raising Stuff.* Enslow Publishers, Inc. ISBN 0766021270.

Greenstein, E. (2003). *Ice-Cream Cones for Sale!* Scholastic, Inc. ISBN 0439327288.

Hale, H. (1997). *Tangrams.* Tarquin Publications, UK. ISBN 0906212561.

Hale, H. (1997). *Pentominoes.* Tarquin Publications, UK. ISBN 090621257X.

Henkes, K. (2003). *Wemberly's Ice-Cream Star.* HarperCollins Children's Books. ISBN 0060504056.

Herman, G. (1996). *The Magic School Bus Blows Its Top.* Scholastic, Inc. ISBN 0590508350.

Hiaasen, C. (2004). *Hoot.* Knopf Publishing. ISBN 0375829164.

Himmelman, J. (2001). *Mealworm's Life.* Scholastic Library Publishing. ISBN 0516272861.

Holderness, J. (2002). *Why Does a Battery Make It Go?* Millbrook Press, Inc. ISBN 0761313384.

Jaffe, E., Labbo, L., & Field, S. (2002). *Dominoes: Games Around the World.* Compass Point Books. ISBN 0756501326.

Jordan, H. (1992). *How a Seed Grows.* HarperCollins Children's Books. ISBN 0064451070.

Kelley, J., & Lugo, M. (2003). *The Little Giant Book of Dominoes.* Sterling Publishing Company, Inc. ISBN 1402702906.

Kline, S. (1989). *Horrible Harry and the Green Slime.* Viking. ISBN 0670824682.

Lankford, M., & Dugan, K. (1998). *Dominoes Around the World.* William Morrow and Company, Inc. ISBN 0688140513.

Lauw, D., & Puay, L. (2001). *Magnets.* Crabtree Publishing Co. ISBN 0778706095.

Lawery, L. (2005). *Cinco de Mayo.* Lerner Publishing Group. ISBN 1575056542.

Learning Resources. (1993). *Problem Solving with Pentominoes.* Learning Resources, Inc. ISBN 1569119996.

Learning Resources. (2005). *Talking Clock.* Learning Resources. ISBN 140063184X.

Learning Resources. (2000). *Try It! Pentominoes.* Learning Resources, Inc. ISBN 1569110573.

Lindman, M. (1995). *Snipp, Snapp, Snurr, and the Buttered Bread.* Albert Whitman. ISBN 0807574910.

Long, L. (1996). *Domino Addition.* Charlesbridge Publishing, Inc. ISBN 0881068772.

Maccarone, G., & Burns, M. (1997). *Three Pigs, One Wolf, and Seven Magic Shapes.* Scholastic, Inc. ISBN 0590308572.

Marsh, V., & Luzadder, P. (1996). *Story Puzzles: Tales in the Tangram Tradition.* Highsmith Press, LLC. ISBN 0917846591.

Mason, A. (2001). Mealworms: *Raise Them, Watch Them, See Them Change.* Kids Can Press, Limited. ISBN 1550745069.

Mitton, T. (2000). *Roaring Rockets.* Houghton Mifflin, Co. ISBN 0753453053.

Moores, E. (2003). *Volcanoes and Earthquakes.* Barnes and Noble Books. ISBN 0760750734.

Neuschwander, C. (2005). *Mummy Math: An Adventure in Geometry.* Holt Henry Books for Young Readers. ISBN 0805075054.

Older, J. (2000). *Telling Time.* Charlesbridge Publishing, Inc. ISBN 0881063975.

Oringel, S., & Silverman, H. (1997). *Math Activities with Dominoes.* ETA/Cuisenaire. ISBN 157452027X.

Pallotta, J. (2003). *Apple Fractions.* Scholastic, Inc. ISBN 043989011.

Pallotta, J., & Bolster, R. (1999). *Hershey's Milk Chocolate Fractions Book.* Scholastic, Inc. ISBN 0439135192.

Pickford, S. (1993). *It's Up to You, Griffin!* Cornell Maritime Press. ISBN 0870334468.

Pistoia, S. (2002). *Fractions.* Child's World, Inc. ISBN 1567661130.

Ralph, J., & Gompf, R. (1995). *Peanut Butter Cookbook for Kids.* Vol. 1. Hyperion. ISBN 0786810289.

Richardson, H. (2001). *How to Build a Rocket.* Scholastic Library Publishing. ISBN 0531139980.

Rockwell, A. (1999). *One Bean.* Walker and Company. ISBN 0802775721.

Rockwell, T. (1977). *How to Eat Fried Worms.* Scholastic Library Publishing. ISBN 0531026310.

Rosinsky, N. (2002). *Magnets: Pulling Together, Pushing Apart.* Picture Window Books. ISBN 140480014X.

Roy, R. (2003). *The School Skeleton.* Bantam Doubleday Dell Books for Young Readers. ISBN 0375813683.

Saunders-Smith, G. (1997). *Beans.* Capstone Press. ISBN 1560654872.

Schaffer, D. (1999). *Mealworms.* Capstone Press. ISBN 0736802096.

Scholastic, Inc. (2004). *I Spy a Rocket Ship.* Scholastic, Inc. ISBN 043945526X.

Schreiber, A. (2003). *Magnets.* Penguin Young Readers Group. ISBN 0448431491.

Seuss, Dr. T. (1976). *Bartholomew and the Oobleck.* Random House, Inc. ISBN 0394800753.

Smith, A. (1990). *Cut and Assemble 3-D Geometric Shapes.* Dover Publications. ISBN 0486250938.

Simon, S. (2002). *Danger! Volcanoes.* North-South Books. ISBN 1587171813.

Sneider, C. (1998). *Oobleck: What Do Scientists Do?* University of California, Berkeley, Lawrence Hall of Science. ISBN 0924886099.

Snyder, I. (2003). *Milk to Ice Cream.* Children's Press. ISBN 0516242687.

Stamper, J. (2003). *Voyage to the Volcano.* Scholastic, Inc. ISBN 0439429358.

Still, D. (2004). *Electricity: Bulbs, Batteries, and Sparks.* Picture Window Books. ISBN 1404802452.

Stillinger, D. (2003). *Battery Science.* Klutz Publishing. ISBN 159174251X.

Taus-Bolstad, S. (2003). *From Milk to Ice Cream: Start to Finish Series.* Lerner Publishing Group. ISBN 0822507145.

Tompert, A. (1997). *Grandfather Tang's Story. Bantam Doubleday Dell Books for Young Readers.* ISBN 0517885581.

Wake, S. (1990). *Butter.* Lerber Publishing Group. ISBN 087614427X.

Wallace, K. (2001). *DK Readers: Rockets and Spaceships.* DK Publishing, Inc. ISBN 0789473593.

Wood, L. (2001). *Volcanoes.* Scholastic, Inc. ISBN 0439295858.

Worth, B. (2001). *Oh Say Can You Seed? All About Flowering Plants.* Random House, Inc. ISBN 0375810951.

Wright, M. (2002). *Telling Time Games: Using the Judy Clock.* Frank Schaffer Publications. ISBN 0768227216.

Resource Book References

Amery, H., Bawden, J., & Butterfield, M. (1993). *Creative Crafts.* Hamlyn Children's Books. ISBN 0679869492.

Chambers, J., Hood, M., & Peake, M. (1995). *A Work of Art.* Belair Publications Limited.

Fiaota, P. (1975). *Snips & Snails & Walnut Whales: Nature Crafts for Children.* Workman Publishing Company. ISBN 0911104496.

Hirshfeld, R., & White, N. (1995). *The Kids' Science Book: Creative Experiences for Hands-On Fun.* Williamson Publishing Co. ISBN 0913589888.

Hume, H. (2000). *A Survival Kit for the Elementary Middle School Art Teacher.* The Center for Applied Research in Education. ISBN 087628456X.

Hyerle, D. (1995). *Thinking Maps: Tools for Learning.* Innovative Learning Group. ISBN 1884582028.

Kohl, M., & Potter, J. (1998). *Global Art.* Gryphon House, Inc. ISBN 087659190X.

McGraw, S. (1991). *Papier-Mâché for Kids.* Firefly Books. ISBN 0920668933.

Merrill, Y. (1995). *Hands-On Celebrations.* Kits Publishing. ISBN 0964317745.

Robins, D. (1993). *Step-by-Step Making Prints.* Kingfisher Books. ISBN 1856979245.

Robins, D. (1993). *Step-by-Step Papier-Mâché.* Kingfisher Books. ISBN 1856979261.

Romberg, J., & Rutz, M. (1972). *Art Today and Every Day.* Parker Publishing Company. ISBN 0130490490.

Ryder, W. (1995). *Celebrating Diversity with Art.* Good Year Books. ISBN 0673361705.

Stickney, L. (2002). *Print-n-Stamp It!* Walter Foster Publishing, Inc. ISBN 1560106514.

Terzian, A. (1993). *The Kids' Multicultural Art Book.* Williamson Publishing. ISBN 0913589721.

Thomson, P. (2002). *Concoct It! Creative Recipes for Crafty Concoctions.* Walter Foster Publishing. ISBN 1560106476.

Trollinger, N. (2002). *Paint It!* Walter Foster Publishing, Inc. ISBN 1560106484.

Website References

English Language Arts

http://www.arcademicskillbuilders.com

www.inknowthat.com

http://www.gamequarium.com

www.literacycenter.net

www.essaypunch.com

http://www.paragraphpunch.com

http://www.spinandspell.com

http://www.spellingtime.com

http://www.apples4theteacher.com/langarts.html

http://www.starfall.com

http://www.tumblebooks.com

http://www.icdlbooks.org

http://www.mightybook.com

http://www.readprint.com

http://www.storylineonline.net

http://www.bookpop.com/index2.html

http://pbskids.org/lions

http://www.saskschools.ca/~ebooks

http://www.bbc.co.uk/schools/typing

http://www.moma.org/interactives/destination

Math

http://www.mathplayground.com

http://www.123techs4me.com/mathmatics.cfm

www.mathforum.com

www.figurethis.org

www.mathcats.com

www.fleetkids.com

www.coolmath4kids.com

http://www.mathforum.com

http://www.aaamath.com

http://www.figurethis.org/index.html

http://www.mathcats.com

http://www.ixl.com

http://www.math.harvard.edu/~knill/mathmovies

http://www.math-drills.com

Science

http://www.chem4kids.com

http://kids.mtpe.hq.nasa.gov

http://kids.nationalgeographic.com/kids

http://school.discoveryeducation.com/index.html

http://www.hhmi.org/coolscience

Social Studies

http://www.pbs.org/teachers/socialstudies

http://www.edhelper.com/Social_Studies.htm

http://www.socialstudiesforkids.com

http://www.proteacher.com/090000.shtml

http://www.50states.com

http://www.teachwithmovies.org

http://www.freerice.com

http://www.dogonews.com

Visual and Performing Arts

http://www.khake.com/page87.html

http://www.getty.edu/education/teachers/index.html

http://www.kinderart.com

http://www.princetonol.com/groups/iad

http://www.kodak.com/global/en/consumer/education/lessonPlans/indices/art.shtml

http://techyteacher.ne/

General Teacher Websites

atozteacherstuff.com *Find lesson plans, thematic units, teacher tips, discussion forums for teachers, downloadable teaching materials, e-books, printable worksheets, emergent reader books, themes, and more.*

edhelper.com *Provides useful educational resources.*

teachertube.com *Provides an online community for sharing instructional videos. Find professional development with teachers teaching teachers and videos designed for students to view in order to learn a concept or skill.*

enchantedlearning.com *Provides teacher resources across the curriculum.*

teacherweb.com *Provides template websites for teachers' use in the classroom. Find customizable and easy-to-use websites that can be created and updated to suit your personal needs in a classroom webpage.*

http://abcteach.com/ *Provides free printable worksheets of all kinds for students pre-K to 8th grade.*